BASIC BRIDGE

Th

This   e top
brid   overs
wan
R   books
and   and
And   fini-
tive   . Set
out   as a
self-   d is
pack
Re   will
conti   dge
for t   be
Basic

b
t
b
v

'One of the best introductory books I have come across is *Basic Bridge*. I recommend it to beginners and teachers alike.'

The European

'*Basic Bridge* is the title of one of the best books for beginners I have seen.'

The Field

BASIC BRIDGE

Ron Klinger

CASSELL
IN ASSOCIATION WITH
PETER CRAWLEY

First published in Great Britain 1994
in association with Peter Crawley
by Victor Gollancz
Eleventh impression 2005
Published in association with Peter Crawley
by Cassell
Wellington House, 125 Strand, London WC2R 0BB
a division of the Orion Publishing Group

A catalogue record for this book
is available from the British Library

ISBN 0 304 35796 0

Typeset in Australia by Modern Bridge Publications,
Northbridge, Australia

Printed and bound in Finland by
WS Bookwell

FOREWORD

When I gave up full-time employment in the field of computing training a few years ago, I started teaching bridge as a way of capitalising on my training background and my years of bridge playing, and as a way of earning a little money. I soon found this was tremendously rewarding and also the most terrific fun. I love the game of bridge and I love bringing its joys to others — even those who I suspect will never advance to become great players!

As a bridge teacher, though, I needed material — reference books to make sure I didn't overlook some of the basics, example hands for students to play, exercises for them to work on and so forth. EBUTA and the indefatigable Pat Husband were a big help and I quickly found the handy Task Master workbooks written by Andrew Kambites and Pat herself to be very useful. I also found myself turning very frequently to the books of Ron Klinger for their clarity of presentation and wealth of examples. In *Basic Bridge*, therefore, I was delighted, as will be countless other bridge teachers and students, to find all three collaborating.

This book would have saved me a great deal of time when I first started teaching bridge. I am sure it will prove a godsend to many others like me in the future.

Christine Duckworth, Manager,
English Bridge Union Teachers' Association

CONTENTS

INTRODUCTION TO THE BRIDGE BEGINNER

Bridge is fun to play but the better you play, the more fun it is. As you improve, you will be fascinated to discover how much there is to the game. Despite popular opinion to the contrary, bridge is not difficult to learn.

This book is the product of many classes given to beginners and improving players. It is intended for those who know nothing about bridge and also for those who know how the game is played but who wish to improve their game. The book can be used as a self-teacher in which case you are advised to follow the recommendations. Alternatively, if used in conjunction with class teaching, follow the recommendations of your chosen teacher if there is a slight difference (e.g., in distribution point count). These are matters of individual opinion rather than right or wrong.

If you are an absolute beginner, it would be worthwhile to play through the games for beginners set out in Pre-Bridge. Then study the chapter headed Mechanics and Rules before starting on Chapter 1.

For the reader who can already play, give plenty of time and thought to the examples, the exercises, the partnership bidding practice and the play hands in each chapter to ensure that you understand the reasoning behind our advice. The aim of this book is to help you feel confident you understand the logic of bidding, card play and defence in bridge : that you can recognise problems and their possible alternative answers and make reasoned decisions. This is the optimum road to the achievement of a sound standard.

It is beneficial to test yourself on the exercises as you progress. You will find it well worthwhile to return regularly to *Basic Bridge* to help you revise. These exercises simulate countless ordinary bidding situations and by scoring well on the exercises, you will build up confidence and also score well at the table when the everyday problems occur.

This book is not for the expert and will not make you an expert bridge player. It does not deal with expert bidding, expert play or expert defence, but it does cover the ordinary, standard situations, *the basics* that make up 95% of the game and in which most ordinary players go wrong. If you follow the recommendations, you will eliminate fundamental flaws from your game and progress from being a novice to becoming a competent, confident bridge player.

Try to play as often as possible. The more you play, the speedier will be your improvement. It is all very well to take lessons and read books, but much of bridge competence is based on experience. The more often you encounter a basic situation, the more readily you will cope with it in future.

Above all, remember that *bridge is a game to be enjoyed.* It can and should be a lot of fun and that is how you should approach it. We hope you derive as much enjoyment and satisfaction from it as we have. *Happy bridging.*

Ron Klinger, Pat Husband and Andrew Kambites, 1994

INTRODUCTION TO THE BRIDGE TEACHER

Bridge classes for beginners usually attract some who have never played before and may lack even basic card knowledge, but in the same group you may find those who have learned socially using little or no formal bidding structure. It is difficult to cater for both groups simultaneously and our recommendation would therefore be to issue a pre-course hand-out to non-card players to introduce them to basic concepts such as the suits, trumps, tricks, etc. or refer them to the material in the section BEFORE Chapter 1 before starting their first class. It is also worthwhile to offer the same pre-reading to those who think they already know how to play.

Pre-Bridge is a game devised as a preliminary to the full intricacies of bridge. This enables students to learn the mechanics of bridge in small, structured steps. The emphasis initially is on declarer play and defence, without which bidding is almost meaningless.

The student practice areas (the exercises, the partnership bidding and the play hands) provide more material than you can usually manage within a lesson. Choose the exercises you feel are most useful but the more student participation the better. Exercises which you have not been able to cover in class can be set as homework and corrected at the start of the next class. Students bring their copy of *Basic Bridge* to each class for the partnership bidding and the play hands.

To minimise latecomers missing new material at the beginning of your class, this useful exercise can start off each of your classes. Construct say a 1NT hand and write it on the board. Have the students set up the hand from the pack of cards on each table. Then let them deal the remaining 39 cards into three hands at random. Have them take each of the random hands in partnership with the fixed 1NT hand and decide how to bid it. You can move from table to table and assist them if they have any problems. After they are familiar with suit bidding, you can start with a fixed one club opening or a one spade opening. Encourage the students to do similar practice at home.

Make sure to include the four play hands in each class. They are at least as important as the main part of the lesson. Students often find this the most valuable part of the lesson and learn much more quickly by playing than by listening. Playing is also more enjoyable and if you can ensure that your students are having a marvellous time, you will have little problem in converting them to bridge for life.

Note that each of the play hands in each chapter is numbered. *At the back of the book, on pages 157-160, you will find the hands for each player also numbered.* Each of these hands refers to the corresponding numbered hand in the text. Using pages 157-160 makes it easy for the students to prepare each of the set deals. The simplest and quickest way is for the pack to be separated into suits in the middle of the table. After you have designated the players as North, East, South, West, each player turns to their page, takes one suit, removes the cards needed for the hand about to be played and returns the rest to the middle of the table. In one or two minutes, each player has taken the cards needed from all four suits and play can now commence.

The hands are structured so that each player is declarer once. Except for the hands on defensive play (Chapter 10), each contract can be made and the idea is to give relatively new players confidence in their ability.

On the page preceding the play hands in each chapter, you will find a section called Tips On Play. Include the tips as part of your lesson since they cover material that crops up in the deals about to be played. This will help some students to do the right thing as declarer.

After the cards have been sorted out, the students should be allowed to bid the hands themselves. After their bidding is finished, go over the bidding with the class and any traps or errors should be explained.

The final contract should be the one in the book, not some other contract the students might have reached. The opening lead is made and corrected if the wrong lead was chosen, together with an appropriate explanation. The students should be left to play the hands on their own, though some brief advice can be given (e.g., 'You need to ruff a club in dummy.'). Students should be encouraged to play the cards in duplicate fashion, so that the hand can be conveniently replayed, if necessary.

Some declarers will go down, some will make overtricks, some defences will be poor. After the hand, spend some time explaining the main thrust of the hand and suggest to the students that they go over the hands at home. Urge them to take a pack of cards, set the hand out suit by suit and then follow the play through trick by trick.

At the end of the course, encourage your students to play as often as possible. If you can arrange supervised practice sessions in conjunction with the course, so much the better. The aim of *Basic Bridge* is to make the game easy and fun for the students and if you can do the same, you will find the teaching of bridge to be a simple, pleasant and rewarding pastime.

Ron Klinger, Pat Husband and Andrew Kambites, 1994

PRE-BRIDGE

WHAT TYPE OF GAME IS BRIDGE?

There are two basic families of card games. In one, the aim is to form combinations of cards, e.g., Gin Rummy, Canasta. Contract Bridge belongs to the other in which the aim is to win tricks. Other games in the trick-taking family are Solo, Five Hundred and Whist.

Bridge is played by four people, two playing as partners against the other two. Partners sit opposite each other. You will need a card table, four chairs, two packs of cards (you can manage with one pack), score pads and pencils.

HOW MANY CARDS ARE IN THE PACK?

A pack (or deck) of 52 cards is used. There are no jokers. There are four suits : spades ♠, hearts ♡, diamonds ◇ and clubs ♣. Each suit has thirteen cards, the highest being the ace followed by the king, queen, jack, 10, 9, 8, 7, 6, 5, 4, 3 down to the 2 which is the lowest.

HOW DO WE CHOOSE PARTNERS?

Partnerships can be by agreement but it is usual to draw for partners. Spread out one pack, face down, and each player picks a card. The two who draw the higher cards play as partners against the other two. If two or more cards of the same rank are turned up, then the tie is split according to suit rank from the highest, spades, through hearts and diamonds, to the lowest, clubs.

WHO DEALS?

The player who drew the highest card has the right to choose seats and which pack of cards to use for dealing, and also becomes the dealer on the first hand. The next dealer will be the player on the left of the previous dealer and so on in clockwise rotation. The cards are shuffled by the player on the dealer's left who passes them across the table to the player on the dealer's right to 'cut' them. The dealer completes the 'cut' and then deals the cards, one at a time, face down in clockwise direction, starting with the player on the dealer's left, until all 52 cards are dealt.

It is customary etiquette not to pick up your cards until the dealer has finished dealing. This allows the dealer the same time to study the cards as everyone else has and also allows a misdeal to be corrected. During the deal, the dealer's partner shuffles the other pack in preparation for the next deal. That is why two packs are used, in order to speed up the game. After shuffling, place the cards on the shuffler's right, ready for the next dealer to pick up.

THE START OF PLAY

After picking up your 13 cards, sort them into suits. It is usual to separate the red suits and the black suits and also to put your cards in order of rank in each suit. The bidding starts with the dealer. More about the bidding later.

PRE-BRIDGE GAME 1 — TRUMPS

Each player receives 13 cards. Opposite players are partners. There is no bidding yet. The top card of the other pack is turned face up. The suit of the face-up card is trumps for that deal. The player on the left of the dealer makes the first lead, that is, places one card face up on the table. Each player plays a card face up in turn, clockwise order. That group of four cards, one from each player, is called a *trick*. *Each player must follow suit if possible.* If you are unable to follow suit, you are permitted to play a trump card which beats any card in any other suit.

A trick with no trump card is won by the highest card in the suit led. A trick with a trump card is won by the highest trump card on the trick. You may play a high card or a low card but you must follow suit if possible. One situation where you could win the trick, but it could be foolish to do so, is if partner's card has already won the trick.

Play continues until all 13 tricks have been played and each side then counts up the number of tricks won. The side winning more than 6 tricks is the winner and is the only side that scores points.

SCORING AT TRUMPS

Spades or Hearts are trumps : 30 points for each trick over six.

Diamonds or Clubs are trumps : 20 points for each trick over six.

The first partnership to score **100 points or more** in tricks won scores a **GAME**. The first game won by each side is worth +300. Winning a second game is worth +500. Play ends when one side wins two games. After play ends, draw for partners and start again.

A bridge score-sheet consists of two columns with a horizontal line a bit more than half-way down. Trick scores are written below the horizontal line, bonus scores go above the line. Your scores go in the left-hand column, theirs in the right-hand column. At the end of a game, a line is ruled across both columns below the tricks score and both sides start the next game from zero again.

At the end of play, both columns are totalled. The side scoring more points is the winner. The difference between the two scores is rounded to the nearest 100 (a difference ending in 50 is rounded down). The score is then entered as the number of 100s won or lost. For example, if you won by 930, your score-sheet reads '+9' while their score-sheet would record '-9'.

GUIDELINES FOR PLAY AT TRUMPS

Prefer to lead a strong suit (headed by a sequence or by A-K) or a singleton. A singleton is a suit with only one-card. When you have no cards left in a suit, you are 'void' in that suit and then you can 'ruff', i.e., trump in. If leading a doubleton (a two-card suit), standard technique is to lead the top card. If you have plenty of trumps, lead trumps to remove the opponents' trump cards so that they cannot ruff your winners.

After a few of these games, move on to . . .

PRE-BRIDGE GAME 2 — NO-TRUMPS

Each player receives 13 cards and the play proceeds as for Game 1 except that there is no trump suit. At no-trumps if a card is led and no other player can follow suit, the card led wins the trick. If you are unable to follow suit at no-trumps, you should discard those cards which you judge to be worthless. Since you cannot win the trick, throw the worst cards away.

SCORING AT NO-TRUMPS

30 points for each trick won over six, plus 10.

1NT (seven tricks) is worth 40, 2NT (eight tricks) = 70, 3NT (nine tricks) = 100, 4NT = 130, and so on.

GUIDELINES FOR PLAY AT NO-TRUMPS

Prefer to lead your longest suit and keep on with that suit. When there is a trump suit, leading a long suit other than trumps has no great advantage since the opponents can soon ruff this suit. At no-trumps, leading a long suit is a powerful strategy because when the others run out, your remaining cards in that suit will be winners. They cannot win the trick if they cannot follow suit and they cannot ruff as there is no trump suit.

Since players tend to lead their own long suit, prefer to return partner's led suit unless you have a strong suit of your own. Usually avoid returning a suit led by the opposition.

Second player to a trick commonly plays low, third player normally plays high. If partner's card has already won the trick, you need not play high. If you can win a trick with a high card, win with the cheapest card possible.

The card to lead from long suits : Start with the top card from a sequence of three or more cards headed by the ten or higher (from K-Q-J-5, lead the K; from J-10-9-4, lead the J).

Lead fourth-highest (fourth from the top) when the long suit has no three-card or longer sequence (from K-J-8-6-3, lead the 6; from J-9-7-2, the 2).

After a few of these games, move on to . . .

PRE-BRIDGE GAME 3 — ENTER THE DUMMY

Each player receives 13 cards and counts the high card points (HCP), using A = 4, K = 3, Q = 2 and J = 1. Starting with the dealer, each player calls out the total number of points held. The side which has more points becomes the declarer side and the partner who has more points becomes the declarer. (The pack has 40 HCP. If each side has 20, redeal the hand. For a tie within the declarer side, the player nearer the dealer is to be the declarer.)

The declarer's partner is known as the 'dummy'. The dummy hand is placed face up on the table, neatly in suits facing declarer. Declarer then nominates ('declares') the trump suit or no-trumps. Choose a trump suit which has 8 or more cards in the combined hands. If more than one trump suit is available, choose a major suit (spades or hearts) rather than a minor suit (diamonds or clubs). The majors score more. If the suits are both majors or both minors, choose the longer. If both have the same length, choose the stronger. With no suit of 8 or more trumps together, choose no-trumps (there is no trump suit).

After the trump suit or no-trumps has been declared, the player on the left of the declarer makes the first lead. The play proceeds as before but **the declarer must play both hands.** The dummy player takes no part in the play. If dummy wins a trick, the next lead comes from dummy, while if declarer wins a trick, declarer must lead to the next trick.

SCORING

If declarer scores seven tricks or more, scoring is as usual. Since the declarer side in this game will have more HCP than the defenders, the declarer side is more likely to succeed in taking seven or more tricks.

It is quite possible that the defenders take more tricks than declarer. If declarer fails to win seven tricks, the opponents score bonus points. Where the declarer side has not previously won a game ('not vulnerable'), the opponents score 50 bonus points for each trick by which they have defeated declarer, regardless of the trump suit or whether no-trumps is played. Where the declarer side has won one game ('vulnerable'), the opponents score 100 bonus points for each trick by which they defeated declarer.

Bonus Points, scored above the line, do not count towards a game. They are valuable since they are included when totalling your points at the end of play. Only the declarer side can score points below the line and only these points, the reward for winning tricks as declarer, count towards the 100 points needed to score a game and collect the game bonus.

The existence of the dummy marks off bridge from other trick-taking games. From the first lead, each player sees half the pack (13 cards in hand and the 13 cards in dummy), thus making Bridge essentially a game of skill in contrast to the large luck factor in the other games.

PRE-BRIDGE GAME 4 — BIDDING

Starting with the dealer, each player states the number of points held. The side with more points is the declarer side and the two partners discuss which suit shall be trumps or whether to play no-trumps. The conversation might start 'How about hearts?' : 'No, what about diamonds?' Each partner in turn suggests a trump suit or no-trumps, until agreement is reached. This is known as the 'bidding' or the 'auction'. A bid simply suggests to partner which suit you prefer as trumps or whether you prefer no-trumps.

A suggested trump suit must contain at least four cards. With no long suit and with no void or singleton it is often best to suggest no-trumps at once. If there is no early agreement and neither partner insists on a suit, one of the partners should suggest no-trumps. After agreement, the first player to suggest the agreed trump suit (or no-trumps, if agreed) is the declarer.

The player on the left of the declarer makes the opening lead *before seeing dummy*. After the lead, dummy's 13 cards are placed face up (in suits) facing declarer (trumps on dummy's right). **Scoring** : Same as for Game 3.

PRE-BRIDGE GAME 5 — MAKING YOUR CONTRACT

Proceed as for Game 4 above, but declarer is required to win a specific number of tricks depending on the total points held by declarer and dummy :

20-22 High Card Points :	7 or more tricks in no-trumps
	8 or more tricks with a trump suit
23-25 High Card Points :	8 or more tricks in no-trumps
	9 or more tricks with a trump suit
26-32 High Card Points :	9 or more tricks in no-trumps
	10 or more tricks with ♡ or ♠ as trumps
	11 or more tricks with ♣ or ◊ as trumps
33-36 High Card Points :	12 or more tricks
37-40 High Card Points :	All 13 tricks

PLAY: The opening lead is made before dummy appears.

SCORING : As for Game 3, but declarer must win the number of tricks stipulated or more. If not, the defenders score 50 (declarer not vulnerable) or 100 (declarer vulnerable) for each trick by which declarer fails.

If required to win 12 tricks the declarer side if successful scores an extra 500 not vulnerable, 750 vulnerable. If required to win all 13 tricks, the declarer side if successful scores an extra 1000 not vulnerable, 1500 vulnerable.

For further information or queries about the correct procedure, see **The Mechanics and Rules Of Bridge** starting on the next page.

THE MECHANICS AND RULES OF BRIDGE
HOW THE GAME IS PLAYED

Bridge is a game for four players, playing in two partnerships. It represents a head-to-head battle — your side against their side. Partners sit opposite each other. Partnerships are chosen by agreement or by lot. Playing social bridge the common method is for each player to choose a card from the pack fanned out face down, with the players selecting the two highest cards as one partnership against the players selecting the two lowest cards.

THE BRIDGE PACK

A regular pack of 52 cards is used and there are no jokers and no cards of any exceptional rank or function (unlike 500 where jacks have a special role, or Canasta where the 2s are jokers).

There are four suits :

♠ SPADES — ♡ HEARTS — ◇ DIAMONDS — ♣ CLUBS

Each suit consists of 13 cards which in order of rank are : Ace, King, Queen, Jack, 10, 9, 8, 7, 6, 5, 4, 3, 2. An ace beats a king, a king beats a queen, a queen beats a jack, a jack beats a ten and so on. The top five cards in each suit (A, K, Q, J and 10) are known as the honour cards or honours.

The suits also have a ranking order : CLUBS (♣) is the lowest suit, then come DIAMONDS (◇) and HEARTS (♡) to the highest ranking suit, SPADES (♠). NO-TRUMPS ranks higher than any suit. The order of the suits - C, D, H, S - is no accident. They are in alphabetical order.

When selecting partnerships, if two cards of the same rank are chosen (e.g., two eights) and the tie needs to be broken, it is decided by suit order (e.g., the ◇8 would outrank the ♣8).

DEALING

The player who drew the highest card is the dealer on the first hand and has the right to choose seats and the pack of cards with which to deal. The next dealer will be the person on the left of the previous dealer and so on in clockwise rotation. In tournament bridge or Chicago, the dealer is specified.

The cards are shuffled by the person on the dealer's left. The dealer passes the pack across the table to the person on the dealer's right to be cut. The dealer then deals the cards, one at a time, face down, in clockwise direction, starting with the player on the left, until all 52 cards are dealt, 13 each.

It is usual to leave your cards face down until the dealer has finished dealing. A misdeal may be corrected if the players have not seen their cards.

While the dealer is dealing, the partner of the dealer is shuffling the other pack in preparation for the next deal. Two packs are used in order to speed up the game. After the shuffling is finished the cards are put down on the shuffler's right, ready for the next dealer to pick up.

THE START OF PLAY

When you pick up your 13 cards, sort them into suits. Separate the red suits and black suits so that you can easily see where one suit ends and the next suit begins.

The bidding starts with the dealer. After the bidding period is over, the side that has bid higher wins the right to play the hand. One member of this side, called the declarer, plays the hand while the opponents defend the hand.

The person on the left of the declarer makes the opening lead. The partner of the declarer now puts all 13 cards face up on the table and arranged in suits. The face up cards are called 'the dummy'. The dummy player takes no part in the play. Declarer plays both hands. Each player can see 26 cards, the 13 in hand plus the 13 in dummy.

Declarer plays one of the cards from dummy, then the third player plays a card and so does declarer. The 4 cards now face up on the table are a 'trick'. A trick consists of 4 cards played in clockwise sequence, one from each hand.

Each deal in bridge is a battle over thirteen tricks, declarer trying to win as many as nominated in the bidding, while the defenders try to win enough tricks to defeat declarer.

The player who wins the trick gathers the 4 cards together, puts them face down neatly and then leads to the next trick, and so on until all 13 tricks have been played. (In tournament bridge, called 'duplicate', the cards are not gathered together. The players keep their own cards in front of them.)

FOLLOWING SUIT

The player who plays the highest ranking card of the suit led wins the trick. If two or more cards of the same rank are played to one trick, who wins then? The basic rule of play is : *YOU MUST FOLLOW SUIT*, i.e., you must play a card of the same suit as the suit led.

If a heart is led, then you must play a heart if you have one and the trick is won by the highest heart played, so that if the two of hearts is led, and the other cards on the trick are the ten of hearts, the queen of spades and the ace of clubs, the trick is won by the ten of hearts.

If you are unable to follow suit, you may play any other card at all but remember it is the highest card of the first led suit which wins. If the king of spades is led, it will do you no good to play the ace of clubs. Only the ace of spades beats the king of spades.

TRUMPS

There is one exception. If, in the bidding, one of the four suits is made the *trump* suit, then any card in the trump suit is higher than any card, even an ace, in one of the other suits. If hearts are trumps, the two of hearts would beat the ace of clubs even when clubs are led. But, first and foremost, you must follow suit. Only when you are out of a suit can you beat a high card of another suit with a trump.

If you are unable to follow suit, you are allowed to trump, *but it is not obligatory.* You may choose to discard, and if, for example, partner has won the trick, it may be foolish to trump partner's winner.

A trick that does not contain a trump is won by the highest card in the suit led. A trick that contains a trump is won by the highest trump on the trick. If you fail to follow suit when able to do so, you have revoked (or 'reneged'). The penalty for a revoke is to transfer one or two tricks to the other side, one trick if you do not win the revoking trick, two tricks if you do win the revoking trick or win a trick later with a card you could have played legally instead of revoking.

THE BIDDING

The play is preceded by the bidding, also called 'the auction'. Just as in an auction an item goes to the highest bidder, so in the bridge auction each side tries to outbid the other for the right to be declarer and play the hand.

The dealer makes the first bid, then the player on dealer's left and so on in clockwise rotation. Each player may decline to bid (say 'No bid') or make a bid. A player who has previously passed may still make a bid later in the auction. A bid consists of a number (1, 2, 3, 4, 5, 6 or 7) followed by a suit or no-trumps, e.g., two spades, three hearts, four no-trumps, seven diamonds. 'No-trumps' means that there is to be no trump suit on the deal.

The number in the bid is the number of tricks to be won *over and above six tricks*. Six tricks is not even halfway and you have to bid for more than half the tricks. The final bid is the 'contract'.

When a bid is made, the bidder is stating the number of tricks above six intended to be won in the play. Add 6 to the number in the bid and that is the number of tricks to be won in the play. The minimum number of tricks that you may contract for is seven. A bid of 1 Club contracts to make seven tricks with clubs as trumps (6 + 1 = 7).

If all players pass without a bid on the first round there is no play, there is no score, the cards are thrown in and the next dealer deals a new hand.

When a player makes a bid on the first round, the auction has started and will be won by the side that bids higher. The auction continues, with each player making a bid or passing, and concludes as soon as a bid is followed by three passes. The side that bids higher sets the trump suit (or no-trumps) and the number of tricks to be won in the play. This is set by the final bid, called 'the contract', and the member of the side who first bid the trump suit (or no-trumps) is the declarer.

After a bid, any player in turn may make a *higher* bid. A bid is higher than a previous bid if it is a larger number than the previous bid or the same number but in a higher ranking denomination. The order of ranking is :

> NO-TRUMPS
> SPADES
> HEARTS
> DIAMONDS
> CLUBS

A bid of 1 Heart is higher than a bid of 1 Club. If you want to bid clubs and the previous bid was 2 Spades, you would have to bid 3 Clubs (or 4 Clubs or 5 Clubs or higher). 2 Clubs would not be higher than 2 Spades.

THE SCORING

It is vital to understand how bridge is scored, for this affects both the bidding and the play. Your aim is to score more points than the opposition.

You may score points :
(1) by bidding and making a contract as declarer
(2) by defeating the opponents' contract
(3) by earning bonus points.

You score points as declarer by bidding and making a contract, according to this table :

NO-TRUMPS	40 points for the first trick (over six) : 1NT = 40
(NT)	30 for each subsequent trick : 2NT = 70, 3NT = 100 . . .
♠ SPADES	30 points for each trick (over six) — *major suit.*
♡ HEARTS	30 points for each trick (over six) — *major suit.*
◊ DIAMONDS	20 points for each trick (over six) — *minor suit.*
♣ CLUBS	20 points for each trick (over six) — *minor suit.*

If declarer makes a contract worth 100 points or more, declarer has made a 'game'. Bonus points are awarded for making a game. *Only the declarer side can score the bonus points for game.* That is the incentive for bidding higher than the opponents.

Since game is 100 points or more, it takes a bid of 5 Clubs or 5 Diamonds to make game in the minors, while a bid of 4 Hearts or 4 Spades or more will score game in the majors. In no-trumps, a bid of 3NT will score a game.

Only points scored by winning the actual number of tricks of the contract count towards the game bonus. A contract score of less than 100 is called a part-score. If you bid 3 Hearts and win ten tricks, you do not score a game. Your part-score contract of 3 Hearts does not score 100 or more. You score 90 for making the nine tricks required for 3 Hearts and score a bonus of 30 points for the extra trick, the 'overtrick'. Whenever declarer makes more tricks than the contract, the overtricks are not lost, but are scored as bonus points.

If declarer fails to make the number of tricks required by the contract, the declaring side scores no points at all, regardless of the number of tricks won. If the contract is 4 Hearts and declarer makes 9 tricks, declarer does not get credit for 9 tricks. The opponents score bonus points for defeating declarer : 50 points for each trick by which declarer fell short if the declarer side is not vulnerable, 100 per trick short if the declarer side is vulnerable.

A small slam is a contract for 12 tricks, a bid of 6NT or 6 in a suit, and a grand slam is a contract for 13 tricks, a bid of 7NT or 7 in a suit. Large bonuses are awarded for bidding and making a slam.

CHICAGO (4-DEAL) BRIDGE

In the 'Chicago' version of bridge, play proceeds in multiples of four deals. Vulnerability is as follows :

> **Deal 1 :** Neither side is vulnerable.

> **Deal 2 :** The dealer's side is not vulnerable, other side vulnerable.

> **Deal 3 :** The dealer's side is not vulnerable, other side vulnerable.

> **Deal 4 :** Both sides are vulnerable.

Part-scores are not carried forward from one deal to the next. For bidding and making a part-score contract, the declarer side scores 50 bonus points in addition to the points for the tricks made. The bonus scores available are :

For a part-score contract :	+50
For a non-vulnerable game :	+300
For a vulnerable game :	+500
For a small slam not vulnerable :	+500
For a small slam vulnerable :	+750
For a grand slam not vulnerable :	+1000
For a grand slam vulnerable :	+1500
For defeating declarer, per trick short	
(a) The declarer side is not vulnerable :	+50
(b) The declarer side is vulnerable :	+100

For details about Doubles and Redoubles, see Chapter 10.

CHAPTER 1

BEFORE THE BIDDING STARTS

THE HIGH CARD POINT COUNT (HCP)

The first thing to do after you have arranged your cards is to estimate how strong your hand is. Count points for your high cards, aces, kings, queens and jacks as follows :

$$A = 4$$
$$K = 3$$
$$Q = 2$$
$$J = 1$$

You will later learn that other points may be added to the high card point total but all hand valuation starts with the 4-3-2-1 count.

HAND PATTERNS AND HAND SHAPES

After you have noted the total HCP, consider the shape of the hand. This is based on the number of cards in each suit.

Each bridge hand contains 13 cards. The pattern of a hand describes the length of each suit in the hand starting with the longest suit, followed by the next longest and ending with the shortest suit. For example, to say that a hand is a 5-4-2-2 means that it contains a 5-card suit, a 4-card suit plus two doubletons, while a 6-3-3-1 pattern means that the hand has a 6-card suit, two 3-card suits and a singleton.

There are three hand shapes: balanced, semi-balanced and unbalanced.

A balanced hand has a 4-3-3-3, 4-4-3-2 or 5-3-3-2 pattern. It contains no void, no singleton and at most one doubleton.

A semi-balanced hand has a 5-4-2-2, 6-3-2-2 or 7-2-2-2 pattern. It contains no void, no singleton, but will have two or three doubletons (in contrast to the balanced shapes which contain either one doubleton or no doubleton).

Unbalanced hands consist of all the other possible patterns which have this common feature: they must contain a void or a singleton. The following table is a summary :

	HAND SHAPES	
BALANCED	**SEMI-BALANCED**	**UNBALANCED**
4-4-3-2	5-4-2-2	4-4-4-1
5-3-3-2	6-3-2-2	5-4-3-1
4-3-3-3	7-2-2-2	and all other shapes
No void, no singleton, at most one doubleton	No void, no singleton, two or three doubletons	which include a void or a singleton

Balanced hands are best for no-trump contracts. Since there is no short suit, at most one doubleton, there is little prospect for trumping and you are bound to follow suit almost throughout the hand. Therefore, a trump contract holds little attraction. Your approach would be to suggest no-trumps early in the bidding.

Unbalanced hands are best for trump contracts. As you hold either a void or a singleton, there is ample opportunity for trumping. Your best approach is to suggest one or more trump suits, agreeing to play no-trumps or suggesting no-trumps only as a last resort.

Semi-balanced hands are reasonable both for trump contracts and for no-trumps. There are two or three doubletons, making trumping attractive, while the absence of any singletons or voids makes no-trumps less risky.

1-SUITERS, 2-SUITERS AND 3-SUITERS

Hands are also described according to how many suits are available for bidding. For a suit to be biddable, it requires at least four cards. When a hand contains only one suit with four or more cards, it is called a one-suiter. When it contains two such suits, it is a two-suiter and with three such suits, it is termed a three-suiter. For example :

1. ♠ 8 6 2	2. ♠ A J 8 7 3	3. ♠ A Q 7 6
♡ A 9 4	♡ K 4	♡ A K J 4
◊ A Q 9 8 3	◊ 8 2	◊ 9
♣ 5 4	♣ A Q J 9	♣ K Q J 9

This is a 10-point, balanced 1-suiter.
Pattern : 5-3-3-2

A 15-point semi-balanced 2-suiter.
Pattern : 5-4-2-2

This is a 20-point, unbalanced 3-suiter.
Pattern : 4-4-4-1

You may also describe the pattern of a hand more precisely by stating the length of the suits in the order spades - hearts - diamonds - clubs. Describing Hand 1 as a 5-3-3-2 does not indicate which is the five-card suit, which is the shortest suit, which are the three-card suits. In exact order, the pattern for hand 1 is 3-3-5-2. Similarly, the pattern for hand 2 is 5-2-2-4 and for hand 3 it is 4-4-1-4.

26

Exercise 1 : Hand shapes

Hands can be balanced, semi-balanced or unbalanced (see previous page). What is the shape of each of these hands?

1. ♠ x x x x
   ♡ x
   ◇ x x x x
   ♣ x x x x

2. ♠ x x x x x
   ♡ x
   ◇ x x
   ♣ x x x x x

3. ♠ x x x x
   ♡ x x
   ◇ x x
   ♣ x x x x x

4. ♠ x x
   ♡ x x x
   ◇ x x x
   ♣ x x x x x

5. ♠ x x x
   ♡ x x x x
   ◇ x x x
   ♣ x x x

6. ♠ x x x x
   ♡ x x x x
   ◇ x x x
   ♣ x x

7. ♠ x x x
   ♡ x
   ◇ x x x x
   ♣ x x x x x

8. ♠ x x x x
   ♡ x x x x
   ◇ x x x x
   ♣ x

Exercise 2 : Points, shape and hand patterns

For each of the following hands, complete these details :

A. High Card Points   **B.** Shape   **C.** Exact Pattern   **D.** 1-, 2- or 3-suiter

1. ♠ A 4
   ♡ Q 8 6 3 2
   ◇ K Q J 9
   ♣ J 2

2. ♠ A K 4 2
   ♡ A 9 8 3
   ◇ K 6
   ♣ 10 4 2

3. ♠ A 9 3
   ♡ Q 9 7 2
   ◇ A Q 4
   ♣ Q 8 2

4. ♠ K J 8 7 6
   ♡ A K J 6 3
   ◇ 6
   ♣ J 8

A. ....

B. ....

C. ....

D. ....

5. ♠ K J
   ♡ 7 5 3
   ◇ A J 9 8 4 2
   ♣ Q 6

6. ♠ A K 9 4 2
   ♡ - - -
   ◇ 6 5
   ♣ A J 8 7 5 2

7. ♠ A 10 9 6
   ♡ 5
   ◇ K J 10 9
   ♣ A Q 10 5

8. ♠ 9 8 6 5 4 2
   ♡ - - -
   ◇ A K 3
   ♣ A Q 8 5

A. ....

B. ....

C. ....

D. ....

POINTS NEEDED FOR GAMES AND SLAMS

IN ORDER TO MAKE		YOU + PARTNER NEED
3NT	9 TRICKS	25-26 points
4 Hearts or 4 Spades	10 TRICKS	26 points + 8 or more trumps
5 Clubs or 5 Diamonds	11 TRICKS	29 points + 8 or more trumps
6-IN-A-SUIT	12 TRICKS	33 points + 8 or more trumps
7-IN-A-SUIT	13 TRICKS	37 points + 8 or more trumps

To say that 25-26 points or more are required to make a game in 3NT, or that 33 points are needed before you should try for a small slam, does not automatically guarantee that you will succeed if you have that number of points. However, the point requirements do mean that with the indicated number of points, you are more likely to succeed than fail. Nevertheless, skill in declarer play may still be required and even with skill you may fail if the cards lie badly for your side. Bridge is not a game of guarantees and certainties. It is a game in which one takes calculated risks. The point requirements reveal when the risks are worth taking, when the odds of obtaining a good score are in your favour.

If you and partner have enough strength to make a game but you fail to bid to a game, you have lost a valuable bonus. Similarly, if the partnership hands can produce a slam but slam is not bid, again a valuable bonus has been lost.

If the opposition bid and make a game, they obtain a valuable score. If you bid higher than their contract, even though you fail, you are better off to bid higher as long as the penalty for defeat is less than the value of their game. The value of a game is usually taken as about 500 points, based on the tricks value and the estimated bonus for the game. It is better to accept a smaller loss (a 'sacrifice') than let the opposition score a game or a slam.

You need not succeed in every game or every slam you bid. The rewards for making a game or a slam are so great that failing now and again is no tragedy and a failure rate in games or slams of about 1 in 4 is normal and expected. Suppose that you bid to 3NT four times and fail on two occasions but succeed on two occasions. Your success rate is only 50% but you are some 700-800 points in front because of the bonus points for winning two games. The point to remember is that you need not be downhearted if you do not make every contract you bid.

The strategy of bidding takes into account the rate of success for game and slam contracts. 3NT with 26 points has about a 60% success rate. With 25 points, the success rate is 50%. As long as you have 8 trumps and 26 points between you, 4♡ or 4♠ has a better success rate, about 80%. Your trump suit protects you against their long suit. Therefore your bidding aims to locate an eight-card or better fit in a major suit as your first objective.

With clubs or diamonds as trumps, if you have eight or more trumps and just 26 points, your chance of making 11 tricks is only 30%. You need 29 points in the minor suits for game to be a good chance. Therefore, if you can tell that your point total is only around 26 points, 3NT has a better chance than 5♣ or 5◊.

The order of priority for games, therefore, is majors first, no-trumps next and minor suits last. However, you do need at least eight trumps for a suit game contract to be worthwhile. If you have only seven trumps between you, the chance of success in 4♡ or 4♠ drops to 40%. Therefore, if you know you have about 26 points but you do not have eight trumps together in a major suit, it is usually wiser to play in 3NT.

TALKING BRIDGE

A little girl is watching her mother and three other ladies playing bridge. As the girl is taking a keen interest in the game, one of the ladies asks her, 'And can you play bridge?' The girl replies, 'No, but I can speak it.'

Bridge players love to discuss bridge hands and there is an accepted method of description. To give a general account of the hand, state the number of high card points held and the hand pattern. For example :

♠ A J 8   A general description would be 'A 16-point 6-3-3-1
♡ 7 3 2   hand.' A more precise description, detailing the pattern
◊ A K Q 9 5 3   by suit lengths in the order of the suits, spades, hearts,
♣ Q   diamonds, clubs would be 'I held a 16-point 3-3-6-1.'

Most players, however, prefer to include the details of the actual high cards held. This is done by stating the honour cards in each suit followed by the total number of cards in that suit. Thus, A-9-6 is 'ace to three', K-Q-5-2 is 'king-queen to four' and A-K-J-8-4-2 is 'ace-king-jack to six'. Where the suit contains no honour cards, the number of cards in the suit is followed by the word 'rags'. Thus, 8-6-2 is 'three rags' and 9-7-4-3-2 is 'five rags'.

If a doubleton is held, use 'doubleton' rather than 'to two' for two specific cards (K-J would be 'king jack doubleton'). For an honour card together with a low card, you can use either 'doubleton' or 'another' after the honour card. Thus, A-4 would be 'ace doubleton' or 'ace-another'. Where the suit has no honour, use 'two rags', 'rag doubleton' or 'doubleton rag'. Where a singleton is held, the terminology is the honour followed by singleton (such as 'king singleton') or, with no honour, 'singleton rag'. It is also common to refer to a singleton honour as 'bare' (such as 'the bare king' or 'king bare').

Specific cards followed by a worthless card are denoted by the word 'another' to mean 'and one worthless card'. Thus, K-Q-3 becomes 'king-queen-another', A-Q-J-4 is 'ace-queen-jack-another', and so on.

The hand above is 'ace jack another, three rags, ace king queen to six and bare queen'.

BRIDGE NOTATION

When writing about bridge, it is conventional to write a bridge bid with the number first, denomination second, just as though it were spoken. Thus, 1NT stands for One No-Trump, 3♠ means Three Spades, 4♡ is a bid of Four Hearts and so on. When writing about cards held or played, the suit symbol is written first followed by the card(s), so that ♠7 stands for the seven of spades, ♡K means the king of hearts, and so on.

When writing a bidding sequence, a colon (:) separates the bids and a comma separates a round of bidding. Bids by your side are written without brackets. For example, 1♡ : 1♠, 2♡ : 4♡ means that your side opened 1♡, responder bid 1♠, opener rebid 2♡ and responder raised to 4♡. The absence of any opposition bids means that they passed throughout.

Bids made by the opposing side are written inside brackets, so for example, 1♠ : (2♣) : Pass : (3♣) . . . indicates that your side opened 1♠, second player overcalled with 2♣, responder passed and fourth player raised to 3♣. Had this been written (1♠) : 2♣ : (Pass) : 3♣ . . . it would show that the opponents had opened the bidding and that it was your side bidding 2♣ and raising to 3♣.

THE ACOL SYSTEM

A bidding system is like a language — it is a means of communicating with your partner. However, the language of bridge allows only 15 legal words : one, two, three, four, five, six, seven, no-trumps, spades, hearts, diamonds, clubs, double, redouble and pass ('no bid'). Without any opposition bidding, there are only 35 bids available between 1 Club and 7 No-Trumps. With this restricted language, you try to describe to partner your thirteen cards, one of billions of possible hands.

A bidding system is not really just one system. It consists of quite a number of sub-systems, each dependent on which opening bid is chosen. The requirements to open the bidding, which opening bid is to be chosen, the requirements to respond and what is meant by each possible response or rebid are stipulated by the system being learnt.

Basic Bridge is based on the ACOL system, one of the most popular bidding systems in the world. It is certainly the easiest to learn and is the most natural of all bidding systems. While you are just starting out at bridge, adopt Acol, stick to it, learn it thoroughly and play it regularly for some two to three years. Once you have become proficient, you may consider adopting modifications to Acol or trying some other system.

In ACOL, as in all systems, bids can be classified and so indicate the intention of the bidder. The main categories are : Limit Bids, Wide-Ranging Bids, Sign-Off Bids, Forcing Bids, Invitational Bids and Conventional Bids.

LIMIT BIDS

A limit bid closely defines the strength and shape of the hand. The most common limit bids are opening bids of 1NT and 2NT. These show a balanced hand (only three patterns possible — see page 26) and the range of High Card Points is usually three at most. In ACOL, the 1NT opening is a balanced 12-14 HCP and the 2NT opening a balanced 20-22 HCP. This makes it very easy for partner to work out the combined strength and most of the time partner can judge the correct contract at once.

ACOL is so accurate because it uses more limit bids than any other system and these limit bids usually occur on the first or second round of bidding. In general, raises of partner's suit, rebids of one's own suit and opening bids, responses and rebids in no-trumps are limit bids.

WIDE-RANGING BIDS

A wide-ranging bid does not have a narrow range of points and the shape is also not closely defined. It is thus the opposite of a limit bid. The most common wide-ranging bids are opening bids of one in a suit and responses or rebids which are a change of suit.

SIGN-OFF BIDS

Often you will know precisely which contract you wish to play. A sign-off bid indicates that the bid you have just made is to be the contract. Partner must not bid again after a sign-off bid. As a limit bid is a very accurate description of the strength and shape of the hand, sign-off bids are very common immediately after a limit bid.

FORCING BIDS

A forcing bid requires partner to bid again. This is not part of the laws of the game but is vital in your bidding strategy. If a bid is forcing, partner may choose any reply but may not pass. If a bid is described as 'not forcing' partner is permitted to pass.

Forcing bids are divided into two groups :

Forcing for one round : If partner makes a bid that is forcing for one round, you are obliged to reply but you need not bid again unless partner makes another forcing bid.

Forcing to game : If a bid is forcing to game, neither partner may pass until a game contract or higher has been reached. This enables the partnership to explore the best game contract or to investigate whether a slam (a contract of 12 or 13 tricks) is possible. After a game-forcing bid has been made, both partners can bid at the cheapest level below game without the fear that partner may pass too soon and bring the bidding to an abrupt end.

INVITATIONAL BIDS

An invitational bid asks partner to keep on bidding if partner has the maximum for the values shown so far and to pass if minimum. Invitational bids often occur just after a limit bid. The limit bid shows a narrow point range but to make an accurate decision, you may still need to know whether partner has the upper end of that narrow range or the bottom end. The solution is to use an invitational bid.

CONVENTIONAL BIDS

Most bidding proceeds as a dialogue of natural bidding. 'Natural' means that any suit you have bid is really held by you and a bid of no-trumps does suggest no-trumps as the contract. For example, if partner starts with One Diamond and you reply One Spade, both bids are natural. Partner will have some diamonds, four at least, and likewise you will have some spades, also four at least.

A conventional bid is an artificial bid, a bid that does not necessarily show the suit bid. In ACOL, for example, the opening bid of Two Clubs is conventional. It is used to show an exceptionally strong hand but the bid has nothing to do with the club suit. It does not promise any minimum number of clubs. You may have some clubs, you may have none. The bid is in no way related to the number of cards you hold in the suit bid and that makes it a conventional bid.

After you have covered the first four chapters, a good exercise is for you and partner to deal out hands at random to practice your bidding. Instead of just making formal bids, add one of the above descriptions after each bid. Thus, your bidding might proceed : 'One No-trump, Limit Bid' : 'Two Spades, Sign-off' or perhaps, 'One Heart, Wide-ranging' : 'Two Clubs, Wide-ranging, forcing for one round.' Regular practice of this kind will help you remember the meaning and purpose behind each of the bids.

CHAPTER 2

BALANCED HAND OPENINGS

The 1NT opening shows 12-14 points and balanced shape.

Most hands in the 12-21 zone start with a suit opening, but if your hand fits 1NT, prefer that opening to any other.

Opening With a Balanced Hand (4-4-3-2 / 5-3-3-2 / 4-3-3-3)

0-11 points : Pass

12-14 HCP : Open 1NT (limit bid). With a 5-3-3-2 pattern, open 1NT if the 5-card suit is a minor. If it is a major, open 1♡ or 1♠.

15-19 points : Open with 1-in-a-suit, 1◇, 1♡, etc. If 4-3-3-3 or 5-3-3-2, open with one of your long suit. If 4-4-3-2, bid your cheaper 4-card suit.

After a 1-level reply : Opener's 1NT rebid (e.g., 1♣ : 1♠, 1NT) =15-16 points. A jump to 2NT (e.g., 1♣ : 1♠, 2NT) = 17-18 and a jump to 3NT = 19.

After a 2-level reply : Opener's 2NT rebid (e.g., 1♡ : 2♣, 2NT) =15-16 points. A jump to 3NT (e.g., 1♡ : 2♣, 3NT) =17-19.

20-22 points : Open 2NT (limit bid) : See Chapter 7.

23 points or more : Open 2♣ : See Chapter 7.

WINNING STRATEGY:

When holding 26 points or more between you and partner, the partnership should bid a game. Therefore, do not pass in the bidding until some game is reached if the partnership *could* have 26 points or more.

With 26 points together, game is a good chance.

With 25 points together, game is a reasonable chance.

With 24 points or less, game prospects are poor.

RESPONDING TO 1NT WITH A BALANCED HAND

0-10 points	PASS	Game prospects poor
11-12 points	2NT (Invitational Bid)	Game possible
13-18 points	3NT (Sign-off)	Strong chances for game
19 points or more	See Chapter 8	Slam is possible
Unbalanced hands	See Chapters 4 & 5	

After 1NT : 2NT (invitational bid), opener should pass with 12 points (minimum) and bid 3NT with 13-14 points (maximum). After 1NT : 3NT (sign-off), opener must pass. After a 1NT or 2NT opening (limit bid), responder makes the decision how high to bid. Responder knows the combined strength, opener does not.

EXERCISES

A. What is your opening bid on these hands?

1. ♠ A 6 2		2. ♠ A Q 6		3. ♠ A Q 6 4 3		4. ♠ K J 6	
♡ K 8 3		♡ K Q		♡ K Q		♡ A Q	
◇ 7 6 5		◇ 7 6 5		◇ Q 6 5		◇ A 10 6 3	
♣ A J 9 4		♣ A J 9 4 2		♣ A J 9		♣ K Q 8 2	

5. ♠ A Q 6		6. ♠ A 9 4 3 2		7. ♠ K Q 6 3		8. ♠ K Q 6 3	
♡ K 9		♡ K 9		♡ K Q 8 2		♡ A Q 8 2	
◇ 7 6 5		◇ 7 6 5		◇ 7 6 5		◇ 7 6 5	
♣ A 9 4 3 2		♣ A Q 6		♣ A J		♣ Q 9	

B. Partner opens 1NT. What is your response?

1. ♠ A 9 8		2. ♠ K 7 6		3. ♠ K 7 6		4. ♠ A K	
♡ K J 7		♡ Q 4 2		♡ 4 3		♡ 7 6 4	
◇ Q 9 8 4		◇ K 9 8		◇ K Q 8 2		◇ Q 9 8	
♣ 7 6 2		♣ A K Q J		♣ Q J 10 3		♣ K J 7 6 2	

PARTNERSHIP BIDDING PRACTICE

West is the dealer on each hand. How should the bidding go?

WEST	EAST	WEST	EAST
1. ♠ A J 7 2	1. ♠ K Q 9	5. ♠ 6 2	5. ♠ A Q 7
♡ A 6 4 3	♡ 9 8	♡ Q 10 6	♡ K J 8 2
◇ 7 5	◇ A K 8 4	◇ K Q J 4	◇ A 7 6
♣ 8 7 2	♣ Q 9 4 3	♣ K 7 4 3	♣ 10 9 5
2. ♠ K Q 8 6	2. ♠ A 3 2	6. ♠ A 3 2	6. ♠ K Q 6
♡ A 9	♡ 10 8 6	♡ A 10 9 2	♡ 8 3
◇ K 6 4	◇ Q J 3 2	◇ K Q 7 2	◇ A J 5
♣ 9 7 6 2	♣ A 10 5	♣ 7 2	♣ A K 6 4 3
3. ♠ A J 4	3. ♠ K Q 3 2	7. ♠ A 3 2	7. ♠ K Q J 6
♡ 8 3	♡ A 9 2	♡ 9 8 7	♡ A 6 2
◇ J 6 3	◇ 8 7 4 2	◇ A J 4	◇ Q 3 2
♣ K Q 7 6 2	♣ A J	♣ A K 6 5	♣ 9 4 3
4. ♠ A 10 9 5	4. ♠ K Q 7	8. ♠ A 9 3	8. ♠ 7 5 2
♡ K Q 7	♡ J 4 2	♡ K 6 2	♡ 9 5 3
◇ K 7 4	◇ A 6 5 3	◇ A 6 4	◇ K Q J 9 5
♣ 8 5 3	♣ Q 6 2	♣ A K J 7	♣ 6 5

TIPS ON DECLARER PLAY

Part 2 deals with principles of declarer play and defence. However, a few tips are given in each bidding chapter to help you cope with the play hands.

For maximum benefit, take a pack of cards and lay out the given cards on the table. Then follow the line of play recommended.

The High-Card-From-Shortage rule

When you have winners in both hands, it is usually best to start with the winners in the shorter hand. For example, with three cards in one hand and four cards in the other, cash the winners first in the three-card holding.

In which order should you play your winners from these combinations? The top hand is always the dummy and the bottom cards are declarer's hand.

1. A J 4	2. A K J 3	3. J 4	4. A J 4 3
K Q 7 2	Q 5	A K Q 10 3	K Q 5

Answers : **1.** Start with the ace, next play the jack and then low to the king.
2. Play the queen first, then the 5 over to dummy's winners.
3. Play the jack first and then the 4 to your winners in hand. If you happen to be in your own hand, lead the 3 to dummy's jack first. High-from-shortage means you also start with low-from-length (the 3 from A-K-Q-10-3) when you are cashing your tricks.
4. Start with the king, then cash the queen and finally lead to dummy's A-J.

Overtaking a winner so that a suit does not become blocked

With plenty of winners in both hands, it may be necessary to overtake a winning card to gain entry to the other hand. Follow the high-card-from-shortage rule and overtake when the last card is played from the shorter length.

How many tricks can you take with each of these combinations? In which order should you play your winners to make all the tricks possible without using an entry in any other suit?

1. A Q	2. A K J	3. K 10 9 5 4	4. K Q
K J 10	Q 10 6 3	A Q J	A J 10 9 8

Answers : **1.** Three tricks possible. Play the ace on the first round, then overtake the queen with your king in order to cash the jack.
2. Four tricks possible. Start with the ace, then the king, then overtake the jack with your queen so that the 10 can be played.
3. Five tricks are available. Play the ace first and the queen next. When you play the jack, overtake it with the king in order to reach dummy's winners.
4. Five tricks. Start with the king, then overtake the queen with the ace.

Note in each case that the maximum number of tricks = the length held in the long hand.

PLAY HANDS FOR THE ONE NO-TRUMP OPENING

(These hands can be made up by using pages 157-160)

Hand 1 : The High-Card-From-Shortage Principle

Dealer North : Nil vulnerable

WEST	NORTH	EAST	SOUTH
	Pass	Pass	1NT
Pass	Pass	Pass	

NORTH
♠ A K J 7
♡ 9 4 3
◇ 8 7 5
♣ 6 4 2

WEST
♠ 10 8 6 5
♡ K Q J 10
◇ K 9 6
♣ J 8

EAST
♠ 9 4 2
♡ 8 5 2
◇ Q J 10
♣ K Q 10 5

SOUTH
♠ Q 3
♡ A 7 6
◇ A 4 3 2
♣ A 9 7 3

Lead : ♡K. Lead the top card from a sequence headed by an honour.

Correct play : After winning the ace of hearts, play the queen of spades (high-from-shortage) followed by a spade to dummy. Cash the other spade winners and your minor suit aces.

Wrong play : Playing a low spade rather than the queen first. If you cash the ace and king of spades, you destroy your queen. If you play low to dummy and then back to your hand, you have two spade winners stranded in dummy.

Hand 2 : High-Card-From-Shortage

Dealer East : N-S vulnerable

WEST	NORTH	EAST	SOUTH
		1NT	Pass
3NT	Pass	Pass	Pass

NORTH
♠ K Q 10 9
♡ 3 2
◇ J 6
♣ 9 8 7 5 4

WEST
♠ 8 7 6
♡ K 6
◇ 9 4 3
♣ A K Q J 2

EAST
♠ A J 3
♡ Q 5 4
◇ A K 5 2
♣ 10 6 3

SOUTH
♠ 5 4 2
♡ A J 10 9 8 7
◇ Q 10 8 7
♣ - - -

Lead : ♡J. With an interior sequence (starting in the middle of a suit), lead the top honour from the sequence.

Correct play : Win the first heart and start on the clubs, playing the 10 from hand and the 2 from dummy (high-from-shortage). Cash the clubs, the ace of spades and ◇A-K.

Wrong play : Failing to win with the ♣10 on the first or second round of clubs. This restricts you to four club tricks because of the 5-0 split and you could go off. The club break is unlucky but by playing correctly, luck is not needed.

Hand 3: Overtaking a winner in order to reach dummy

Dealer South : E-W vulnerable

NORTH
♠ 7 5 4 3
♡ Q J 10 9
♦ K Q 10
♣ 10 6

WEST
♠ Q J
♡ 6 3 2
♦ J 8 5 2
♣ A K Q J

EAST
♠ A K 10 2
♡ A 4
♦ 6 4 3
♣ 8 5 3 2

SOUTH
♠ 9 8 6
♡ K 8 7 5
♦ A 9 7
♣ 9 7 4

WEST	NORTH	EAST	SOUTH
			Pass
1NT	Pass	2NT	Pass
3NT	Pass	Pass	Pass

Lead : ♡Q. Top of sequence. With equal length, lead the stronger suit.

Correct play : After winning ♡A, lead a low spade to the queen in hand (high-from-shortage). Continue with the ♠J and overtake with dummy's king or ace. Cash the spade and club winners.

Wrong play : (1) Playing the ♠A or ♠K on the first round of spades.
(2) Failing to overtake the second round of spades with dummy's ace or king. This would leave two spade winners stranded in dummy.

Hand 4 : Overtaking a winner to gain access to dummy

Dealer West : Both vulnerable

NORTH
♠ J 9 2
♡ A K 2
♦ K Q J
♣ 8 6 3 2

WEST
♠ A 6 4
♡ 10 9 8 5
♦ 8 4
♣ A 10 7 5

EAST
♠ 10 8 7 5 3
♡ Q 7 6
♦ 9 7 2
♣ K 9

SOUTH
♠ K Q
♡ J 4 3
♦ A 10 6 5 3
♣ Q J 4

WEST	NORTH	EAST	SOUTH
Pass	1NT	Pass	3NT
Pass	Pass	Pass	

Lead : ♠5, fourth-highest. West should win ♠A and return a spade.

Correct play : Lead a diamond to the king, cash the ♦Q and then overtake the ♦J with dummy's ace. Cash the diamonds and then the hearts and the jack of spades. 9 tricks.

Wrong play : (1) Failing to overtake the third round of diamonds. This allows the defence to defeat 3NT.
(2) Playing the ♦A on the first or second round of diamonds. This will 'block' the diamonds and leave two diamond winners stranded in dummy.

CHAPTER 3

OPENING THE BIDDING WITH HANDS THAT ARE UNBALANCED OR SEMI-BALANCED

When you open with a suit bid, you will have either a balanced hand with 15 points or more (you would open 1NT with 12-14 balanced) or a hand that is unbalanced or semi-balanced.

When valuing for a suit opening, count high card points and add :

LENGTH POINTS

1 point for each 5-card suit, 2 points for a 6-card suit, and so on. Points are used to measure trick-taking potential. Just as tricks can be won with high cards, so a long suit provides potential for extra winners. The longer the suit, the greater the likelihood of more winners from that suit.

When Should You Open?

0-11 points : Do not open with a one-bid. With a long, strong suit, your hand may be worth a pre-emptive opening of 3, 4 or 5 (see Chapter 9).

12-22 total points : With an unbalanced or a semi-balanced hand, open with a bid of one in a suit. The one-opening should include at least 10 high card points. With a balanced hand, see Chapter 2 for the correct opening.

Hands with maximum points may be suitable for a two-opening if a long, strong suit is held (see Chapter 7).

23 points or more : Choose a two-opening (see Chapter 7).

Which Suit Should You Open?

(1)   Open the longest suit.

(2)   With two 5-card suits or two 6-card suits, open the higher-ranking.

(3)   With no 5-card suit, your hand pattern must be a 4-4-4-1 if the hand is not balanced. The 4-4-4-1s are rare (only about 3% of all hand patterns) but if you do pick up a 4-4-4-1 which is worth an opening bid of one :

● **With a red singleton, start with the suit below your singleton.**

● **With a black singleton, start with the suit in the middle.**

EXAMPLES

1. ♠ A Q J 6	2. ♠ A Q 6 4	3. ♠ Q 6 5 3 2	4. ♠ A Q 6 4 3
♡ K Q 8	♡ A K 8 3	♡ K Q J 8 4	♡ - - -
◇ 7 6 5 4 3	◇ 7	◇ 7	◇ K 5
♣ J	♣ 8 6 4 2	♣ A J	♣ Q J 6 4 3 2

Open 1◇.	Open 1♣. Below	Open 1♠. Higher	Open 1♣.
Longest suit first.	the red singleton.	suit with 5-5s.	Longest suit first.

EXERCISE

What is your opening bid on these hands?

1. ♠ A Q 6 3	2. ♠ Q	3. ♠ A K Q 2	4. ♠ J 8 6 3
♡ K Q 8 2	♡ A 9 8 2	♡ 9	♡ A Q 10 2
◇ A J 6 5	◇ A 7 6 5	◇ A 7 6 5	◇ 5
♣ 4	♣ A 7 3 2	♣ 8 7 4 3	♣ A K 9 6

5. ♠ Q 9 6	6. ♠ Q J 6 5 4 3	7. ♠ J 8 4 3 2	8. ♠ K 6 3
♡ A K	♡ A K 9 5 4	♡ A K Q J	♡ Q 8 7 4 2
◇ 6 5	◇ 7	◇ Q 7 5	◇ 7
♣ A J 9 4 3 2	♣ 2	♣ 2	♣ A K Q 9

9. ♠ J 6	10. ♠ 6 3	11. ♠ Q 6 4	12. ♠ A K 8 6 2
♡ A Q 4 2	♡ 2	♡ A Q	♡ 9
◇ 5 3	◇ A Q 9 5 3	◇ A 7 6 5	◇ A 7
♣ K 9 6 5 3	♣ K Q 9 7 6	♣ A 7 3 2	♣ K Q 6 5 3

13. ♠ K 6 3 2	14. ♠ - - -	15. ♠ Q J	16. ♠ 4 3 2
♡ Q 8 7 4	♡ A K	♡ A K 9 5	♡ 3 2
◇ A K	◇ 9 6 5 4 3 2	◇ A 5	◇ A Q 9 3
♣ A K Q	♣ A J 9 4 3	♣ Q 7 5 4 2	♣ A K 9 7

17. ♠ 7	18. ♠ 7 6 4	19. ♠ Q J 6 3	20. ♠ Q 3
♡ A Q 9 5	♡ A Q J	♡ K Q	♡ A 9 2
◇ A 7 6 5	◇ K Q J	◇ A K 6 5	◇ A 7 6 5 3
♣ 9 6 5 4	♣ A K J 2	♣ A K Q	♣ K 9 2

21. ♠ J 4 3 2	22. ♠ K 6 3	23. ♠ 8 6 5 4 3 2	24. ♠ A Q 4 3
♡ - - -	♡ Q 8 7 5 2	♡ A K	♡ A J
◇ K Q 10 4	◇ - - -	◇ K J	◇ K J 7 2
♣ A J 8 6 2	♣ A K 6 3 2	♣ A 9 3	♣ A 4 3

TIPS ON DECLARER PLAY

For maximum benefit, take a pack of cards and lay out the given cards on the table. Then follow the order of play recommended.

Setting up extra winners

With holdings such as K-Q-4 opposite J-3-2, where you have all the vital high cards bar the ace, you can set up extra tricks by leading the suit and using one of your high cards to force out the ace. When faced with a choice of cashing winners or setting up extra tricks, it is almost always better to set up the extra tricks first, cash your certain winners later. If the length in dummy and in your hand is not equal, lead the high card first from the shorter holding (an extension of the high-card-from-shortage rule).

How many tricks can you take with each of these combinations? In which order should you play your high cards?

1. Q 4 3	2. K J 5	3. J 10 5 4	4. K Q 4 3
K J	Q 10 4 3	K Q 6 3	J 10 5

Answers : **1.** Two tricks. Start with the king. Next time play the jack.
2. Three tricks. Start with the king. Next time play the jack.
3. Three tricks. The order does not matter when you have the same number of cards in each hand. The only decision you need to make is where you wish to have entries later in the play. If entries to dummy are needed, start with the king and queen. If entries in your own hand are more useful, play the jack and ten on the first two rounds.
4. Three tricks. Play the jack first, the ten next time.

Likewise where your card combination includes the queen, jack and ten you can set up a trick by forcing out their king and ace.

How many tricks can you take with each of these combinations? In which order should you play your high cards?

1. Q 4	2. Q J 5	3. 10 9 8 4 2	4. A 6
J 10 9 2	10 4 3	Q J 3	Q J 10 5

Answers : **1.** Two tricks. Start with the queen. If the lead is in your own hand, play the 2 to the queen. Next time play the jack. After the king and ace have gone, you are left with two winners.
2. One trick. The order does not matter since you have the same number of cards in each hand. You may start with the ten first or play one of dummy's honours first.
3. Three tricks. You need to dislodge their ace and king. Start with the queen. Next time lead the jack.
4. Three tricks. Play the ace first (high card from shortage) and then lead the 6 to your queen. If the king takes this, your jack and ten are winners.

BALANCED HANDS TOO STRONG TO OPEN 1NT

(These hands can be made up by using pages 157-160)

Hand 5 : High-from-shortage — Setting up an extra winner

Dealer North : Nil vulnerable

WEST	NORTH	EAST	SOUTH
	Pass	Pass	1♣
1◊	1♠	Pass	1NT
Pass	Pass	Pass	

NORTH
♠ A J 7 2
♡ Q 5 3
◊ 9 4 2
♣ J 6 2

WEST
♠ 10 4 3
♡ A 8
◊ K Q J 10 7
♣ Q 7 4

EAST
♠ 9 6 5
♡ J 10 9 4 2
◊ 8 5
♣ K 10 5

SOUTH
♠ K Q 8
♡ K 7 6
◊ A 6 3
♣ A 9 8 3

Bidding : South's 1NT rebid shows 15-16 points and a balanced hand.

Lead : ◊K. Top of sequence.

Correct play : After winning the ace of diamonds, play the king-queen of spades (the high-from-shortage rule) and a spade to dummy to cash the ace and jack. Then lead a heart to the king. When the ace takes this the queen in dummy is a winner.

Wrong play : If you cash the ace of clubs before leading a heart, you can be defeated.

Hand 6 : Setting up extra tricks before cashing winners

Dealer East : N-S vulnerable

WEST	NORTH	EAST	SOUTH
		Pass	Pass
1♣	Pass	1♡	Pass
2NT	Pass	3NT	All pass

NORTH
♠ K 10 5
♡ 8 7 5
◊ Q J 8 6 2
♣ 7 4

WEST
♠ 8 7 6
♡ K Q 3
◊ A 4 3
♣ A K Q 2

EAST
♠ A 3 2
♡ J 10 4 2
◊ K 9 5
♣ 10 6 3

SOUTH
♠ Q J 9 4
♡ A 9 6
◊ 10 7
♣ J 9 8 5

Bidding : West's jump rebid to 2NT shows 17-18 points and balanced.

Lead : ◊6. Fourth-highest is normal if your long suit has no sequence of *three* cards or more headed by an honour.

Correct play : Start with the heart king to set up 3 heart tricks. South should win and return a diamond (partner's suit). Win, cash the heart queen and a lead a heart to dummy. If you cash your club, diamond and spade winners before playing hearts, the defence has enough tricks to beat you. Set up the extra tricks first.

Hand 7 : Setting up extra tricks before cashing winners

Dealer South : E-W vulnerable

NORTH
- ♠ A K
- ♡ 10 6 2
- ◇ Q J 10 9
- ♣ A Q 7 2

WEST
- ♠ 10 7 4
- ♡ Q J 9 7
- ◇ K 7 5
- ♣ 10 6 4

EAST
- ♠ Q J 5 2
- ♡ 5 4
- ◇ A 4 3
- ♣ J 9 8 5

SOUTH
- ♠ 9 8 6 3
- ♡ A K 8 3
- ◇ 8 6 2
- ♣ K 3

WEST	NORTH	EAST	SOUTH
			Pass
Pass	1♣	Pass	1♡
Pass	1NT	Pass	3NT
Pass	Pass	Pass	

Bidding : North's 1NT = 15-16. South counts 25-26 points together.

Lead : ♠2. Fourth-highest. Do not choose a club lead. Avoid leading a suit bid by the opponents.

Correct play : After winning ♠A, lead the ◇Q. Say West wins and plays another spade. Win this and lead the ◇J. If they cash two spades, you can discard one heart and one club.

When playing the clubs, start with the king (high-from-shortage).

Hand 8 : Setting up extra tricks — Keeping an entry to dummy

Dealer West : Both vulnerable

NORTH
- ♠ K J 10 8 2
- ♡ 9 8 7
- ◇ Q 9
- ♣ Q 10 8

WEST
- ♠ 9 6 4
- ♡ Q J 10 2
- ◇ A 2
- ♣ 7 6 3 2

EAST
- ♠ A 7 5
- ♡ A 6
- ◇ K J 4 3
- ♣ A K 9 5

SOUTH
- ♠ Q 3
- ♡ K 5 4 3
- ◇ 10 8 7 6 5
- ♣ J 4

WEST	NORTH	EAST	SOUTH
Pass	Pass	1♣	Pass
1♡	Pass	3NT	All pass

Bidding : East's 3NT rebid shows 19 points and a balanced hand.

Lead : ◇6. Fourth-highest. Not the ◇8. Top of sequence applies only when you are leading an honour.

Correct play : Play low in dummy and capture North's queen. If the ◇Q were with South, East's jack would win. East thus has three diamond tricks. Continue with the ace of hearts and another heart. This sets up two extra tricks in hearts. Note that the ◇A is needed as your entry to the established heart winners.

Set up extra tricks before cashing winners. If East plays the ♠A first, the defence can defeat 3NT.

CHAPTER 4

RESPONDING WITH WEAK HANDS

RESPONDING TO AN OPENING OF 1♣, 1◊, 1♡ OR 1♠

0-5 total points : Pass. In counting your points, use the 4-3-2-1 count for the ace, king, queen, jack plus your length points (one point for each card beyond four in a suit). Thus, 5 HCP and a 5-card suit = 6 points and is worth a response. So is 4 HCP and a 6-card suit.

6-9 total points : Bid, but only at the 1-level *or* raise the opener's suit to the 2-level. Even though you may have a weak hand, game is still possible when partner starts with a 1-opening in a suit, as partner can have as much as 20 points or even a bit more. **Therefore, always respond to a suit bid with 6 points or more.** Do not be concerned just because you have a weak hand. It is not what *you* have that matters. It is what the partnership holds that indicates how high you should bid.

When responding with a weak hand, it is important to keep the bidding at a low level initially, since partner may have only a minimum opening of around 12-13 points. Then the partnership may have only about 19-20 points, perhaps a little more. With the strength evenly divided between the two sides, it will be tough for you to make more than 7 or 8 tricks. Consequently, you may raise opener's suit to the 2-level with a weak hand, but otherwise you must remain at the 1-level. *You are not entitled to bid a new suit at the 2-level with 6-9 points, only with 10 total points or more.*

Your Choice of Response : Raise Opener *or* Bid A New Suit *or* Bid 1NT

Raise opener to the 2-level : 6-9 points + support for opener's suit.

A decent trump holding for your partnership is 8 trumps or more. With fewer than 8 trumps, the opponents will have almost as many as you or more than you. This makes your task to win very difficult. Since the partnership should have at least 8 trumps, you should have four trumps (or more) to support opener's suit which need be no more than a 4-card suit.

When you do have trump support for partner, value your hand by counting the high card points and adding on points for the short suits where you might win tricks by ruffing. The ruffing point count when supporting partner is :

The 5-3-1 count : 5 for a void, 3 for a singleton, 1 for each doubleton.

When you assess your hand originally count HCP + Length Points. After a trump fit is established switch to counting HCP + Ruffing Points. *Do not count both Length Points and Ruffing Points.* Count one or the other.

Length Points are appropriate when you are planning to play in no-trumps or where there is not a trump fit. Ruffing Points are more accurate when a trump fit exists. At least eight trumps together are needed. Do not count Ruffing Points until you know that a suitable trump fit is available.

The 5-3-1 Ruffing Point Count is a way of estimating the tricks you will win with one or more of your low trumps by ruffing. These low trumps may not otherwise take a trick. With a void you are quite likely to win two tricks by ruffing. With a singleton, at least one ruffing trick is likely. Tricks by ruffing are usually independent of tricks won with high cards. Therefore we count points for the high cards and also points for probable ruffing tricks.

Respond 1NT : 6-9 points, no support for opener, no suit at the 1-level.

If unable to raise opener and unable to bid a suit at the 1-level respond 1NT as your last resort. Because of the importance of the rule requiring 10 total points for a new suit at the 2-level, the 1NT response need not be balanced. Do not choose the 1NT response if you have a 4-card or longer suit that can be bid at the 1-level. *The 1NT response denies holding a suit that could have been bid below 1NT.* The 1NT response to 1♣ shows 4 very poor clubs and a 4-3-3-3 pattern.

Bid Your Own Suit (but only at the 1-level) : 6 points or more.

The suit you bid must contain at least four cards but it need not have any high cards in the suit itself. In other words, any 4-card suit is biddable.

A significant difference between bidding your own suit at the 1-level and raising opener to the 2-level or responding 1NT is this : while the raise is 6-9 and the 1NT response is 6-9, the new suit response is 6 points *or more.* In other words, a new suit at the 1-level might be based on a strong hand, which you will reveal later in the bidding, but it need not have more than the minimum of 6 points. Because the raise to the 2-level is limited (6-9) and the 1NT response is limited (6-9), opener may pass these responses, but since a new suit response is unlimited (6 points or more), opener is obliged to rebid after a new suit response.

What if you have a choice of suits?

Where you have a choice of suits as responder, the order of bidding your suits is the same as for opener :

● Bid your longest suit first.

● With two 5-card suits or two 6-card suits, bid the higher-ranking.

● With two or three 4-card suits, bid the cheapest suit first.

'Cheapest' means the first available bid over partner's bid, not necessarily the lowest-ranking suit. If partner opened 1♡ and you have 4 spades and 4 clubs, 1♠ is a cheaper bid than 2♣. Likewise, if partner opened 1◇ and you hold 4 spades and 4 hearts, the cheaper suit is hearts and your response should be 1♡. This method of bidding your cheapest 4-card suit is called bidding your suits 'up-the-line'. Note that 'up-the-line' applies only to 4-card suits, *not to 5-card suits.*

The above order of preference in bidding suits is subject to the overriding priority that *you should not bid a new suit at the 2-level unless you have at least 10 points.* Consequently, when you have only 6-9 points, you may occasionally be forced into bidding a suit which is not your normal first preference. Suppose partner has opened 1◇ and you have only 6-9 points with 4 spades and 5 clubs. You should respond 1♠. Your hand is not strong enough for 2♣. That would promise 10 points *or more.*

Resolving a Choice of Responses

What happens when your hand fits two or more responses? Perhaps you are able to support partner but you also have a suit of your own? Perhaps you could raise opener, bid your own suit or respond 1NT?

The way to solve such conflicts will depend on whether your partner has opened with a major suit or with a minor suit. If you have only 6-9 points, this is the order of responding priorities :

If partner opened with a major suit :

1. Raise opener's major.

2. Bid 1♠ over 1♡ if unable to support hearts.

3. Respond 1NT.

If partner opened with a minor suit :

1. Bid a new suit at the 1-level.

2. Raise opener's minor.

3. Respond 1NT.

These priorities apply when responding with a weak hand. There may be different priorities when responding with a strong hand (see Chapter 5).

When changing suit in response to an opening bid of 1♣ or 1◇, you should follow the normal rules when you have a choice of suits : bid your longest suit first; bid the higher suit with two 5-card suits or two 6-card suits, and bid up-the-line with 4-card suits. In reply to a 1♣ opening, with club support and a diamond suit as well (but no major), choose the club raise unless the diamonds are longer or much stronger than your clubs.

EXERCISES

A. Partner opened 1♣, next player passed. What is your response?

1. ♠ K J 8 2	2. ♠ A K 8	3. ♠ A 9 8	4. ♠ A 7 6 3
♡ A 7 6	♡ 9 6 2	♡ 9 6 2	♡ Q 8 4 3
◊ 9 6 4	◊ 8 7 6 3	◊ 6 3 2	◊ J 5
♣ 8 7 3	♣ 6 3 2	♣ K 7 6 3	♣ 6 4 2
5. ♠ A Q 9 7	6. ♠ A Q 9 7	7. ♠ K 8 7 4 3	8. ♠ 3
♡ 9 3	♡ 9 3	♡ A 8 7 4 2	♡ K 8 7 4 3
◊ K 8 6 5	◊ 8 6 3	◊ 3	◊ 5 2
♣ 8 6 3	♣ K 8 6 5	♣ 5 2	♣ A 8 7 4 2

B. Partner opened 1♡, next player passed. What is your response?

1. ♠ K 7 6 4	2. ♠ 8 7 5 4	3. ♠ K 7	4. ♠ K 7 6
♡ 8	♡ 8 2	♡ 6 2	♡ 2
◊ Q 9 7 2	◊ A K 7	◊ Q 9 7 4	◊ Q 9 7 4
♣ Q 8 4 3	♣ J 8 4 3	♣ Q 8 4 3 2	♣ Q 8 4 3 2
5. ♠ A 7 5	6. ♠ A J 9 7	7. ♠ A 8 7 3 2	8. ♠ 7
♡ J 7 3 2	♡ Q 9 8 3	♡ Q J 4 2	♡ 9 7 5 2
◊ 9 7	◊ 7 4 2	◊ 9 4	◊ 10 9 4 2
♣ 8 6 5 2	♣ 4 2	♣ 6 2	♣ A 7 4 2

C. What is your response on these hands if partner opened . . .

(a) 1 Club?   (b) 1 Diamond?   (c) 1 Heart?   (d) 1 Spade?

The player on your right has passed partner's opening bid.

1. ♠ J 4 3 2	2. ♠ K J 8 3	3. ♠ Q J 6 5 2	4. ♠ K 7 6 2
♡ 8 6	♡ 6 2	♡ K 3	♡ 9 8 4 3
◊ A J 7 4 3	◊ Q J 6 3	◊ 8 7 3	◊ 5
♣ 9 5	♣ 7 6 4	♣ 9 4 2	♣ K 8 6 4
5. ♠ A Q 8 3	6. ♠ Q 9 7 4 3	7. ♠ 4 3	8. ♠ 3
♡ 8 7 6 2	♡ 6	♡ A J 7 6	♡ Q 8 7 4
◊ 7 5	◊ A 7 6 5 4 2	◊ 6 2	◊ K J 5 2
♣ 4 3 2	♣ 4	♣ Q 10 7 5 4	♣ 9 7 4 3

Shut-out Jump-Raises

The jump-raises to game in the major suits (1♡ : 4♡ and 1♠ : 4♠) are used on weakish responding hands. They show about 6-9 high card points (could possibly be less), 5 or more trumps and unbalanced shape (must have a singleton or a void). The message is : 'I have excellent support but am weak in high cards.' They are called 'shut-out' because their function is to shut the next player out of the bidding. At the same time they serve as a warning to partner not to expect too much in high cards if partner has notions about a slam. They are also sometimes called 'gambling raises', but with the excellent support and unbalanced shape, it is not much of a gamble.

Shut-out raises in the minor suits (1♣ : 4♣ *or* 1♣ : 5♣ *or* 1◊ : 4◊ *or* 1◊ : 5◊) are available but are very rare since they by-pass a possible 3NT contract. When used, however, they do show the same sort of hand as the shut-out raise in the major suits, namely weak in high cards (usually 6-9 high card points, occasionally even weaker), 5-card or longer trump support and an unbalanced hand (must contain a void or a singleton).

RESPONDING TO AN OPENING BID OF 1NT

Responding to 1NT with a balanced hand was covered in Chapter 3.

Responding to 1NT with a weak unbalanced hand is different to responding to a suit opening, because the 1NT opening is a limit bid, a balanced 12-14. The suit opening has a wide range, 12-21 points and balanced, semi-balanced or unbalanced shape. You would pass a suit opening with 0-5 points but you are allowed, even encouraged, to respond to 1NT if you have a long suit, even with a hopelessly weak hand. The weaker the hand and the fewer the entries, the more important it is to play with your long suit as trumps.

♠ Q J 9 8 4 3
♡ 7
◊ Q 8 6
♣ 4 3 2

Partner opened 1NT. Your response?
This hand is far more powerful in spades than in no-trumps. It is conceivable that in no-trumps your hand takes no tricks. With spades as trumps, you should score four tricks at least. Bid 2♠.

1NT: 2-in-a-suit = Sign-off, 0-10 points and a 5-card or longer suit.

Opener must pass this 2-level response.

1NT : 2♣ is commonly used as the Stayman Convention which you should certainly adopt after you have played for some time (see Appendix 1).

With 11 points or more, responder has a chance for game opposite 1NT and therefore must not make a weak suit response at the 2-level. 2NT is used as an invitational response with exactly 11-12 points (see Chapter 3) and the Stayman Convention (see Appendix 1) can also be used when exploring for game in a major suit with 11 points or more. Other strong responses to 1NT are covered in Chapter 5.

SUMMARY TABLE OF WEAK RESPONSES

(L = Limit Bid, W-R = Wide-range, S-O = Sign-off, F = forcing, NF = Not forcing)

OPENING	SEQUENCE	EXPECTED HOLDING
1♣	1♣ : 1◊ W-R, F	6+ points, 4+ diamonds
	1♣ : 1♡ W-R, F	6+ points, 4+ hearts
	1♣ : 1♠ W-R, F	6+ points, 4+ spades
	1♣ : 1NT L, NF	6-9 points, 3-3-3-4 pattern, poor clubs
	1♣ : 2♣ L, NF	6-9 points, 4+ clubs, no major
1◊	1◊ : 1♡ W-R, F	6+ points, 4+ hearts
	1◊ : 1♠ W-R, F	6+ points, 4+ spades
	1◊ : 1NT L, NF	6-9 points, no 4-card major
	1◊ : 2◊ L, NF	6-9 points, 4+ diamonds, no 4-major
1♡	1♡ : 1♠ W-R, F	6+ points, 4+ spades, no 4 hearts
	1♡ : 1NT L, NF	6-9 points, no 4-card major
	1♡ : 2♡ L, NF	6-9 points, 4+ hearts
	1♡ : 4♡ L, NF	Below 10 HCP, 5+ trumps, unbalanced
1♠	1♠ : 1NT L, NF	6-9 points without spade support
	1♠ : 2♠ L, NF	6-9 points with spade support
	1♠ : 4♠ L, NF	Below 10 HCP, 5+ trumps, unbalanced
1NT	1NT : 2♣	Stayman Convention (see Appendix 1)
	1NT : 2◊ S-O	0-10 points, 5+ diamonds. Opener must pass.
	1NT : 2♡ S-O	0-10 points, 5+ hearts. Opener must pass.
	1NT : 2♠ S-O	0-10 points, 5+ spades. Opener must pass.

OPENER'S REBIDS AFTER A WEAK RESPONSE

Opener's hand is generally divided into three ranges :

        12-15 points : **Minimum opening**

        16-18 points : **Strong opening**

        19 points up : **Maximum opening**

Strategy : If the partnership may hold 26 points, keep on bidding since game is feasible. If the combined total is 25 points at least and there might be more, bid for a game. If the combined total is 24 points at most and there might be less, do not bid for a game. With 26 points together, game is a good bet; with 25 points together, game is a reasonable bet and with 24 points or less together, game is a poor bet. This bidding strategy is revealed in the approach taken by opener after a weak response from partner.

After a raise of opener's suit to the 2-level (e.g., 1♡ : 2♡, . . .?)

Count HCP plus 5-3-1 shortages (void 5, singleton 3, doubleton 1).

12-15 points	**Pass** (responder has 6-9 = no 25 points.)
16-18 points	**Bid again** (raise a major to the 3-level; if your suit is a minor, raise to the 3-level or try 2NT.)
19 points up	**Bid game** (if your suit is a major, raise to the 4-level; if it is a minor, consider 3NT if your hand is balanced or semi-balanced.)

After a 1NT response (e.g., 1♡ : 1NT, . . . ?)

(a) If satisfied with no-trumps :

12-15 points	**Pass** (responder has 6-9 = no 26 points.)
16-18 points	**2NT** (opener may be balanced or semi-balanced.)
19 points up	**3NT** (the partnership has 25 points at worst.)

(b) If not happy with no-trumps :

12-15 points	Bid a new suit lower than your first bid suit *or* repeat your first suit with extra length in the suit.
16-18 points	Bid any new suit *or* with no second suit, jump to three in the first suit with 6 cards in it.
19 points up	Jump to the 3-level in a new suit (jump-shift) *or* jump to game in your suit.

♠ A 9 8 4 3
♡ A 9 7
◇ K Q
♣ J 3 2

You opened 1♠. Your rebid after 2♠ or 1NT?
Over 2♠ you should pass — the partnership does not have 26 points. Pass also over 1NT. A 5-3-3-2 is a balanced shape and so no-trumps is attractive.

♠ 7
♡ A 9 7 3 2
◇ K Q 8 6
♣ Q J 4

You opened 1♡. Your rebid after 2♡ or 1NT?
Over 2♡, you should pass — no 26 points — but over 1NT, prefer 2◇. Your hand is unbalanced and so a trump contract figures to be a better chance.

♠ A Q 8 6 4
♡ A K 9 3
◇ A Q
♣ J 7

You opened 1♠. Your rebid after 2♠ or 1NT?
You have more than 20 points and therefore enough for game opposite partner's 6-9 points. Over 2♠, bid 4♠.
Over 1NT, bid 3♡ (jump-shift) forcing to game.

♠ 9
♡ K Q 8
◇ A K 8 7 4 3
♣ A 9 3

You opened 1◇. Your rebid after 2◇ or 1NT?
Game is possible but not certain. In both cases, rebid 3◇ to invite game. Responder will pass if minimum, but will bid again with a maximum (8-9 points).

After a suit response at the 1-level (e.g., 1♣ : 1♡, . . .?)

(a) Opener has 12-15 points

With a minimum opening, opener makes a minimum rebid. You must not make a jump rebid as opener unless you have a strong hand. In order of preference, opener's possible rebids are :

● **Raise responder's suit.** This requires 4-card support since the suit bid by responder need not have more than four cards in it. Opener would not raise responder's suit at once if the bidding has started 1♣ : 1◇ and opener has a 4-card major as well as support for diamonds. Show your major first rather than support partner's minor.

● **Bid a new suit at the 1-level.** The new suit must have four cards in it, but any suit quality will do. Prefer to bid a new suit at the 1-level to rebidding with 1NT or repeating your first suit. **The Skip-Over Principle :** If opener by-passes a suit with the rebid, opener denies four cards in that suit. For example, 1♣ : 1◇, 1NT denies four hearts and denies four spades.

● **Rebid 1NT.** This shows a balanced hand with 15-16 points.

● **Bid a new suit at the 2-level lower than your first suit.** With a minimum opening, you should not rebid higher than two of your first suit unless you are supporting responder's suit.

● **Rebid your first suit.** To rebid your suit after a 1-level response, the suit must have extra length (more than the opening promised).

(b) Opener has 16-18 points

In order of preference, opener should :

● **Jump-raise responder's suit to the 3-level.** Opener must have 4-card support for this. The only time opener would not raise responder at once is if the bidding has begun 1♣ : 1♢, and opener has a 4-card major as well as support for diamonds. In that case, show the major first.

● **Bid a new suit at the 1-level or 2-level.**

● **Jump to 2NT (17-18 points), provided that your hand is balanced.** With 15-16 points, the rebid would be 1NT (see previous page).

● **Jump to the 3-level in the suit opened with at least 6 cards in that suit.**

(c) Opener has 19 points or more

In order of preference, opener should :

● **Jump to game in responder's major suit.** This requires 4-card support. If the bidding has started 1♣ : 1♢, opener would rather bid a 4-card major than jump to game in diamonds (which requires 11 tricks). In that case, opener would jump-shift to two of the major rather than support the diamonds yet. Majors come first.

● **Jump-shift (i.e., make a jump bid in a new suit).** The jump-shift denies a balanced hand but is forcing to game as it promises 19 points up.

● **Jump to 3NT with 19 points and a balanced hand.** After 1♣ : 1♢, prefer a 3NT rebid with a suitable hand rather than a raise of diamonds.

● **Jump to game in the suit opened with a very powerful 6-card suit (it should contain at least four honours) or a strong 7-card suit.**

♠ Q 8	You opened 1♢. Your rebid after 1♡ or 1♠ ?
♡ 4 2	In either case you should rebid 2♣, showing your
♢ A J 8 7 3	second suit and denying a balanced hand (no NT rebid).
♣ A K J 6	Further action will depend on responder's rebid.

♠ A K 3	You opened 1♣. Your rebid after 1♢, 1♡ or 1♠?
♡ A Q 4	In each case rebid with a jump to 2NT showing a
♢ A 9 8	balanced 17-18 points. Responder may pass, bid 3NT,
♣ J 10 3 2	suggest a suit contract or aim for slam.

♠ A 7 3 2	You opened 1♢. Your rebid after 1♡ or 1♠?
♡ 6	Over 1♡, rebid 1♠ and not 2♢. Show a major rather than
♢ A Q J 9 5	rebid a longer minor. Over 1♠, you are worth 17 points
♣ K 8 3	(via the singleton) so that you should jump-raise to 3♠.

REBIDDING AFTER A ONE-OVER-ONE SUIT RESPONSE

N.B. Opener must not pass. Describe your hand as best you can.

(L = Limit Bid, W-R = Wide-range, S-O = Sign-off, F = forcing, NF = Not forcing)

TYPE OF ACTION	SAMPLE AUCTION	SHOWING	FORCING?
Raise Responder			
Simple raise	1♦ : 1♠ 2♠	L : Minimum hand (12-15) and 4-card support	Not forcing
Jump raise	1♦ : 1♠ 3♠	L : Strong hand (16-18) plus 4-card support	NF, but bid game with 8+ pts
Game raise	1♦ : 1♠ 4♠	L : Super hand (19+ pts.) plus 4-card support	NF but consider slam prospects
Bid a new suit			
At the one-level	1♣ : 1♥ 1♠	W-R : 12-18 points, at least 4-4 in the suits bid	NF but almost never passed
At the two-level (i) Lower-ranking	1♥ : 1♠ 2♣	W-R : 12-18 points, first suit usually 5+ cards	NF but bid on with 8+ points
(ii) Higher-ranking	1♦ : 1♠ 2♥	16+ points, first suit is 5+ and longer than second	Forcing for one round
Jump shift	1♣ : 1♥ 2♠	Super hand, 19+ points	Forcing to game
Bid no-trumps			
1NT	1♦ : 1♠ 1NT	L : 15-16 points, balanced, denies support	Not forcing
2NT	1♦ : 1♠ 2NT	L : 17-18 points, balanced, denies support	Not forcing
3NT	1♦ : 1♠ 3NT	L : 19 points, balanced and denies support	Not forcing
Rebid own suit			
Cheapest rebid	1♥ : 1♠ 2♥	L : Minimum hand, 12-15, and usually 6+ suit	Not forcing
Jump rebid	1♥ : 1♠ 3♥	L : Strong hand, 16-18, plus good 6+ suit	NF but bid game with 8+ points
Game rebid	1♥ : 1♠ 4♥	L : Super hand, 19+ points and self-sufficient suit	NF but consider slam prospects

RESPONDER'S REBID WITH A WEAK RESPONDING HAND

If the opener has made a minimum rebid, confirming a hand in the 12-15 point range, responder is allowed to pass. However, responder is not obliged to pass, but responder with a weak hand must not make a strong rebid. Responder is entitled to bid again with a weak hand, provided that responder's rebid is :

● **A raise of opener's second suit** (e.g., 1♣ : 1♡, 1♠ : 2♠). This still shows just 6-9 points in the same way that an immediate raise (1♠ : 2♠) shows 6-9 points. Four trumps are needed to raise opener's second suit.

● **A preference to opener's first suit** (e.g., 1◊ : 1♡, 1♠ : 2◊). This also shows just 6-9 points in the same way that an immediate raise of opener's first suit (1◊ : 2◊) shows 6-9 points.

● **A rebid of 1NT shows 6-9 points in the same way that an initial response of 1NT shows 6-9 points.**

● **As a last resort, responder may rebid his own suit, provided that it contains at least six cards or is a strong 5-card suit.**

If opener's rebid is a jump showing 16-18 points, the responder is permitted to pass with just 6-7 points but is expected to bid on with 8 points or more since the partnership could then have 26 points or better.

If opener's rebid is a change of suit, opener may have up to 18 points (opener's range for a change of suit is 12-18 since 19 points or more are needed for a jump-shift rebid). Accordingly, responder strives to find a rebid with 8 points or better, since the partnership could have 26 points.

If opener's rebid is a jump showing 19 points or more, responder is forced to bid again if game has not yet been reached (e.g., 1♠ : 1NT, 3♡), but is permitted to pass, of course, if opener's rebid is already a game (e.g., 1♡ : 1♠, 4♡).

♠ A J 8 7 6 ♡ 7 3 2 ◊ K 5 4 ♣ 8 6	Partner opened 1◊, you responded 1♠. Now, if partner rebids 1NT, 2◊ or 2♠, you should pass but if partner rebids 2♣, rebid 2◊. Show a preference for one of partner's suits rather than rebid an ordinary 5-card suit.
♠ A 10 9 7 3 2 ♡ Q 4 ◊ 2 ♣ 8 7 5 3	If partner opened 1◊ and you responded 1♠, then if partner rebids 1NT, 2◊ or 2♡, you should rebid 2♠, showing long spades but a minimum response (6-9 points) but if partner rebids 2NT or 3♠, you should rebid 4♠.

PARTNERSHIP BIDDING PRACTICE
FEATURING RESPONDING WITH WEAK HANDS

West is the dealer on each hand. How should the bidding go?

WEST	EAST	WEST	EAST
9. ♠ K Q 7 4	9. ♠ 6 5	16. ♠ A J 8 7 6	16. ♠ 5 2
♡ A 8	♡ K J 5 2	♡ A K Q 3	♡ J 9 7 6
◊ Q 7 3	◊ K 8 6 4	◊ A J	◊ K 6 4 3
♣ A 7 6 2	♣ 8 5 3	♣ 7 6	♣ K 8 4
10. ♠ K 8	10. ♠ A J 4 3 2	17. ♠ K 7 2	17. ♠ A J
♡ A 9 3 2	♡ K 8 6 5	♡ A 8 3	♡ K Q 9 7 2
◊ K 6 2	◊ 3	◊ 9 5 4	◊ A J 6 2
♣ A K 6 2	♣ 7 4 3	♣ Q 6 5 3	♣ 8 7
11. ♠ A K 4	11. ♠ 7 2	18. ♠ 4	18. ♠ A 10 9 5 3
♡ 8 3	♡ K Q J 6 4 2	♡ J 8 3	♡ K Q 7 2
◊ A K 3 2	◊ 6 5	◊ J 6 3 2	◊ K 7
♣ K Q 8 6	♣ 7 4 2	♣ K Q 7 6 2	♣ 8 5
12. ♠ K Q 9	12. ♠ 6 2	19. ♠ Q 10 5	19. ♠ A K J
♡ 9 8	♡ Q 7 6	♡ Q J 6	♡ K 9 2
◊ A K 8 2	◊ Q J 4 3	◊ 8 2	◊ K J 7 6 3
♣ Q J 6 3	♣ K 7 4 2	♣ Q 9 5 4 3	♣ 8 2
13. ♠ 3	13. ♠ A 6 4	20. ♠ A 5 2	20. ♠ J 6
♡ Q 10 8 6 3	♡ A 5 2	♡ A 5 3	♡ 8 6
◊ Q J 3 2	◊ K 7 4	◊ J 9 5	◊ K Q 8 4 3 2
♣ K 9 5	♣ A Q J 2	♣ A K 6 5	♣ 10 7 3
14. ♠ Q 4 3	14. ♠ A 9 7 2	21. ♠ Q 8 3 2	21. ♠ J 9 7 4
♡ A 6 2	♡ K Q 4	♡ K Q 9 5	♡ 7 4 3
◊ 10 7 5 4 2	◊ K 8	◊ 9 4	◊ A J
♣ 4 2	♣ K Q J 5	♣ 8 4 3	♣ A K Q 2
15. ♠ 9 7 6 4 2	15. ♠ A K 5 3	22. ♠ A J 7 5	22. ♠ K 9 8 3
♡ 7 5	♡ A 9 3	♡ 4	♡ 8 7 6 5 2
◊ A 8 5 4	◊ 6	◊ K 4 3	◊ Q J 5
♣ J 9	♣ A K 8 4 3	♣ A K Q 5 2	♣ 4

TIPS ON DECLARER PLAY

Drawing trumps

When playing a trump contract it is usually correct to draw trumps as soon as possible. Your aim is to remove their trump cards so that they cannot win tricks with them by ruffing your winners later.

```
              NORTH
              ♠ A 7 6 3
              ♡ Q 6 3
              ◇ A K 2
              ♣ J 7 3
WEST                      EAST
♠ 10                      ♠ J 9 8
♡ 8 5                     ♡ J 10 9 4 2
◇ Q J 10 8 7 5            ◇ 9
♣ A Q 4 2                 ♣ K 10 9 6
              SOUTH
              ♠ K Q 5 4 2
              ♡ A K 7
              ◇ 6 4 3
              ♣ 8 5
```

North opens 1NT, South jumps to 3♠ and North raises to 4♠. West leads the queen of diamonds. How should South play?

This is a straightforward hand. Win the lead and play spades, A, K, Q, to remove their trumps. Then play your heart winners and the other diamond winner. Ten tricks.

If you do not play trumps early, you may fail. Suppose declarer wins and plays three rounds of hearts first. West ruffs the third heart and leads the jack of diamonds. East ruffs dummy's honour and 4♠ is beaten by two tricks.

That is the main purpose of drawing (removing) the enemy trumps. You can play your winners later in safety.

To count trumps, start by working out how many trumps the opponents hold. Then after each round, deduct the trumps they have played to see how many are still missing. On the hand above, South would think : 'I have five trumps, dummy has four. That's nine. So they have four trumps.' After the first round of trumps : 'Right. They played one each, so there are still two trumps missing.' After the second round : 'Aha, West did not follow, so only one of their trumps went on that round. East still has one trump left.' That is one simple bit of arithmetic each round. It is more efficient than stopping after each round and counting the number you have left, the number left in dummy and the trumps already played and deducting from 13.

In some cases you will start drawing trumps and find that there is one trump still missing and higher than any of your trumps. Most of the time it pays you to leave that top trump out and move on to your next best suit.

Sometimes it is necessary to delay drawing trumps. If dummy has few trumps and you need to ruff losers in dummy, you may need to ruff the losers before removing dummy's trumps. In other situations, playing trumps may lose the lead. If you have too many losers and the opponents can cash these tricks when they obtain the lead, it may be necessary to discard losers before starting trumps. The hands that follow illustrate these problems.

PLAY HANDS ON WEAK RESPONDING HANDS

(These hands can be made up by using pages 157-160)

Hand 9 : Drawing trumps — Discarding a loser on dummy's winner

Dealer North : Nil vulnerable

NORTH
♠ A K Q 9 8 3
♡ A 8 6
◇ Q 3
♣ J 10

WEST
♠ 10 2
♡ 4
◇ K 10 7 6
♣ 8 7 6 5 4 2

EAST
♠ J
♡ K Q J 10 5 3
◇ A J 8 2
♣ 9 3

SOUTH
♠ 7 6 5 4
♡ 9 7 2
◇ 9 5 4
♣ A K Q

WEST	NORTH	EAST	SOUTH
	1♠	2♡	2♠
Pass	3♠	Pass	4♠
Pass	Pass	Pass	

Bidding : North's 3♠ invites South to bid game with 8-9 points.

Lead : ♡K, top of sequence.

Play : North wins ♡A, draws trumps in two rounds and plays A, K, Q of clubs to discard a red suit loser. It is normal to draw trumps first.

Wrong play : (1) Failing to win the ♡A at trick one. West would ruff the next heart and 4♠ could be beaten.
(2) Playing clubs before drawing trumps. East ruffs the third round of clubs and 4♠ would be beaten.

Hand 10 : Drawing trumps — Setting up winners to discard a loser

Dealer East : N-S vulnerable

NORTH
♠ 10 6
♡ 8 2
◇ 9 8 4 3
♣ K 10 6 4 2

WEST
♠ K J 9 8
♡ 6 5 4
◇ J 5
♣ J 8 7 3

EAST
♠ A Q 4 3
♡ A K 7
◇ K Q 10 7 2
♣ 9

SOUTH
♠ 7 5 2
♡ Q J 10 9 3
◇ A 6
♣ A Q 5

WEST	NORTH	EAST	SOUTH
		1◇	1♡
1♠	Pass	4♠	All pass

Bidding : West is worth the 1♠ response and East revalues to 21 points, counting 3 for the singleton, since support is held for West's suit.

Lead : ♡8. Lead partner's suit. From a doubleton, lead the top card.

Play : Win the ♡A. Draw trumps in three rounds. Next play the jack of diamonds to knock out the ace and so set up the other diamonds as winners. When the lead is regained, play the diamonds and discard a heart loser and two clubs. Set up a long suit before playing to ruff losers.

Hand 11: Ruffing a loser in dummy — Drawing trumps delayed

Dealer South : Both vulnerable

WEST	NORTH	EAST	SOUTH
			1♥
Pass	1NT	Pass	3♥
Pass	Pass	Pass	

NORTH
♠ 5 3
♥ 9 2
♦ K Q 9 3
♣ J 8 7 4 2

WEST
♠ Q J 10 8
♥ Q J 5
♦ 5 4 2
♣ K 6 3

EAST
♠ 7 6 4 2
♥ 10 7
♦ A J 10 8
♣ A 10 9

SOUTH
♠ A K 9
♥ A K 8 6 4 3
♦ 7 6
♣ Q 5

Bidding : South's 3♥ shows six hearts and 16-18 points, inviting North to bid game with more than 6-7 points.

Lead : ♠Q. Top of sequence.

Play : South should win and play the other spade winner, followed by the third spade, ruffed in dummy. Next, the A-K of hearts should be followed by a diamond to the king.

Wrong play : Failing to ruff the spade loser in dummy. If South plays A-K of hearts at once, dummy is unable to ruff a spade and there are five losers.

Hand 12 : Urgent discard of losers — Drawing trumps delayed

Dealer West : Nil vulnerable

WEST	NORTH	EAST	SOUTH
1♣	Pass	1♥	1♠
2NT	Pass	3♦	Pass
3♥	Pass	4♥	All pass

NORTH
♠ 5 4
♥ 8 6
♦ A 10 9 3
♣ 10 7 5 4 2

WEST
♠ A 9 8
♥ K 4 2
♦ Q 8 6
♣ A K Q 3

EAST
♠ 7 3 2
♥ Q J 10 9 5
♦ K J 7 2
♣ 6

SOUTH
♠ K Q J 10 6
♥ A 7 3
♦ 5 4
♣ J 9 8

Bidding : 2NT = 17-18 points. East's 3♦ shows 5 hearts - 4 diamonds at least and so West prefers hearts.

Lead : ♠K. Top of sequence.

Play : Win ♠A. Play ♣A, K, Q to discard two spade losers. Then lead trumps. When the lead is regained, draw the missing trumps, followed by diamonds to knock out the ◊A. After winning ♠A, you have four losers. If you lead trumps at trick 2, South wins and cashes two spades and you will go one down.

CHAPTER 5

RESPONDING WITH
STRONG HANDS

RESPONDING TO AN OPENING OF 1♣, 1◊, 1♡ OR 1♠

Hands with 10 or more high card points are considered strong hands for responder. 10 HCP and 4-card support for opener would be too strong for a single raise to the 2-level. 10 HCP would also be too strong to respond 1NT. Note that 9 HCP with a 5+ suit and 8 HCP with a 6+ suit are valued as 10 total points and so these are likewise treated as strong hands.

Responder's most common action with a strong hand is to change suit, await further information from opener and then either make a decision as to the best contract or make another descriptive bid to help partner. When responder is changing suit, the normal order of priorities applies :

- Bid your longest suit first.

- With 5-5 or 6-6 patterns, bid the higher-ranking suit first.

- 4-card suits are bid up-the-line.

Since responder has a strong hand, there will not be any need to bid the suits out of natural order. Responder might have to bid suits in a different order with a weak hand (see page 45). When bidding a new suit, responder may bid at the 1-level or at the 2-level. At the 1-level a new suit shows 6 points or more. A new suit at the 2-level shows 10 points or more, provided that it is not a jump-shift. When bidding a new suit, responder bids at the cheapest possible level and a suit response at the 1-level does not deny a strong hand. If responder does jump-shift (e.g., 1♣ : 2♡ *or* 1♠ : 3♣), responder shows 16 points or more and usually a powerful 5-card or longer suit. The jump-shift is rare. It forces to game and suggests slam possibilities.

Aside from changing suit, responder has three specific strong responses, but the hand must fit the requirements before these bids are chosen :

- 2NT response — 11-12 points, balanced shape, stoppers in unbid suits.

- 3NT response — 13-15 points, 4-3-3-3 pattern, stoppers in unbid suits.

- Jump-raise, e.g., 1♠ : 3♠ — 10-12 with 4-card support for opener.

Responder's general strategy of developing a strong hand :

With 4-card support for opener's major and 10-12 points, choose the jump-raise (e.g., 1♡ : 3♡). If partner's opening was 1♣ or 1◊ and you have support for the minor suit and a major suit as well, choose the change of suit response. The raise of a minor suit denies a major.

If the hand fits 2NT or 3NT, choose the no-trump response as long as you do not have a 4-card major. With a major, choose the change of suit response. A 2NT or 3NT response denies a major. The minimum holdings which qualify as stoppers are A-x, K-x, Q-x-x or J-x-x-x.

With most hands in the 10-12 point range, respond with a change of suit and then bid again, inviting game. For example, 1♠ : 2♣, 2◊ : 3◊ . . . *or* 1♡ : 2♣, 2◊ : 2NT . . . A change of suit at the 2-level has already shown 10 points. If followed by support of opener's suit or 2NT or a rebid of responder's suit, the range is limited to 10-12 points. If you changed suit at the 1-level, you still show 10-12 points if, after opener's minimum suit rebid, you follow up with 2NT or raise opener to the 3-level or rebid your own suit at the 3-level (e.g., 1◊ : 1♡, 1♠ : 2NT . . . *or* 1◊ : 1♡, 1♠ : 3♠).

With 13-15 points, responder has enough for game and on almost all 13-15 hands (those that do not fit the 3NT response), responder should start with a change of suit. On the next round you may bid game if you know the best spot (for example, 1◊ : 1♠, 2♣ : 4♠) or change suit again which will require the opener to bid once more (for example, 1♡ : 2♣, 2♡ : 2♠ . . .).

With 16 points up, choose a jump-shift response to show a powerful 5-card or longer suit (e.g., 1♠ : 3◊ *or* 1♣ : 2♡). Use the jump-shift on one-suiter hands or hands with a strong suit as well as support for opener's suit. For the vast majority of hands with 16+ points, change suit initially and decide on game or slam chances after you hear opener's rebid. If still uncertain, you can force opener to keep bidding by a second change of suit.

An opening hand facing an opening hand should produce a game.

An opening hand facing an opener who jumps can produce a slam if a good trump fit is located. A 19-up hand opposite an opening will usually produce a slam if a good trump fit is located.

RESPONDING TO A 1NT OPENING

With 13 points or more opposite a 1NT opening, game is a good bet. Jump directly to game if you know the best spot (e.g., 1NT : 4♠). Jump to 3-in-a-suit (e.g., 1NT : 3♡) to force to game and show a 5-card suit. Opener will support your suit if possible, but with only a doubleton, opener rebids 3NT. You may also use the Stayman Convention (see Appendix 1) with 11 points or more and a 4-card major. As game is possible if responder has 11 points or more, do not respond to 1NT with 2-in-a-suit which shows only 0-10 points. With 11-12 points only and a long minor or both minors, stick to no-trumps.

♠ A Q 8 6 4 Suppose partner opens 1♣. You know you have enough for
♡ A K 9 5   a game, but which game? As you cannot tell, respond 1♠
◇ 7 3 2   and await opener's rebid. Over 2♠ bid 4♠, but over 2♣ bid
♣ 5   2♡, a new suit and forcing. Over 1NT, jump to 3♡, forcing.

♠ A Q J 9 8 2 If partner opens 1♣, respond 1♠. Then, over 2♠, rebid 4♠.
♡ A 9 3   Over 1NT rebid 4♠, as opener will have 2-3 spades. The
◇ 7 3 2   1NT rebid shows 15-16 points and a balanced hand. Over
♣ 5   2♣ rebid 4♠ also, a reasonable gamble with strong spades.

♠ A J 5   If partner opens the bidding, you have enough for a game
♡ Q 9 6   no matter which opening bid was made. You are worth
◇ K J 8   3NT, showing 13-15 points, stoppers in the unbid suits and
♣ Q J 9 4   a 4-3-3-3 pattern with no 4-card major.

♠ 8   If partner opens the bidding 1♠, respond 2♡, the higher suit
♡ A 9 8 5 4   with a 5-5 pattern. Normally, responder's change of suit
◇ A Q 7 4 3 promises no more than a 4-card suit. However, 1♠ : 2♡
♣ J 2   *promises five hearts or more* and is an exception.

♠ A 7 5 2   If partner opens 1♡, respond 1♠. 4-card suits are bid up-
♡ 5   the-line whether opening or responding. 'Cheapest' suit does
◇ A J 6 3   not mean 'lowest' suit. 1♠ is cheaper than 2♣. 2NT would
♣ Q J 9 4   be a serious error since that guarantees a balanced hand.

♠ A J 8   Over a 1♣ opening, jump to 3♣ and over 1◇, jump to 3◇.
♡ 8 7   You are much too strong just to raise to the two-level. Over
◇ Q J 6 4   a 1♡ opening, this hand is worth 2NT, while after a 1♠
♣ K 9 8 3   opening, respond 2♣, bidding your 4-card suits up-the-line.

♠ A K Q J 7 4 If partner opens the bidding with 1♣, 1◇ or 1♡, you should
♡ A K 8   respond 2♠, a jump-shift showing 16 points or more. This is
◇ 8 7   forcing to game and suggests a slam is possible. The jump-
♣ 8 2   shift normally shows a strong 5-card or longer suit.

♠ 8 5   If partner opens 1♠, your hand is ideal for a 2NT response,
♡ Q 9 4 2   while over 1♡, you should jump-raise to 3♡. Over 1♣ or
◇ A 8 7   1◇, your spades are too weak for a response of 2NT. In
♣ K Q 5 4   either case, it is best to start with a response of 1♡.

♠ A J 8   After partner opens the bidding, you have enough for a
♡ A 9 8 5   slam but which slam? Simply change suit and await
◇ A K J 3   partner's rebid. You will have a better idea where you
♣ K 2   should finish after you have heard more from opener.

SUMMARY TABLE OF STRONG RESPONSES

(L = Limit Bid, W-R = Wide-range, S-O = Sign-off, F = forcing, NF = Not forcing)

OPENING BID	SEQUENCE	EXPECTED HOLDING
1♣	1♣ : 3♣	L, NF, 10-12 pts, 4+ clubs, no major
	1♣ : 2NT	L, NF, 10-12 points, balanced hand with no major, stoppers in unbid suits
	1♣ : 3NT	L, NF, 13-15 points, 4-3-3-3 pattern with no major, stoppers in unbid suits
	1♣ : 2♦/2♥/2♠	W-R, 16+ points, 5+ suit, game force
1♦	1♦ : 2♣	W-R, 10+ points, 4+ clubs, forcing
	1♦ : 3♦	L, NF, 10-12 pts, 4+ trumps, no major
	1♦ : 2NT	L, NF, 10-12 points, balanced hand with no major, stoppers in unbid suits
	1♦ : 3NT	L, NF, 13-15 points, 4-3-3-3 pattern with no major, stoppers in unbid suits
	1♦ : 2♥/2♠/3♣	W-R, 16+ points, 5+ suit, game force
1♥ or 1♠	1♥ : 2♣/2♦ 1♠ : 2♣/2♦	W-R, F, 10+ points, 4+ suit
	1♠ : 2♥	W-R, F, 10+ points, *five or more* hearts,
	1♥ : 3♥ 1♠ : 3♠	L, NF, 10-12 points, 4+ trumps
	1♥ : 2NT 1♠ : 2NT	L, NF 10-12 points, balanced hand with no major, stoppers in unbid suits
	1♥ : 3NT 1♠ : 3NT	L, NF, 13-15 points, 4-3-3-3 pattern, no 4-major, stoppers in unbid suits
	1♥ : 2♠/3♣/3♦ 1♠ : 3♣/3♦/3♥	W-R, 16+ points, 5+ suit, game force
1NT	1NT : 2♣	Stayman Convention (see Appendix 1) asking for opener's 4-card major
	1NT : 3♣/3♦ 1NT : 3♥/3♠	W-R, game force, 5+ suit, 13+ points, counting Length Points
	1NT : 4♥/4♠	S-O, 6+ suit, 13+ points counting LP

EXERCISES ON RESPONDING WITH A STRONG HAND

A. Partner opens 1♣, next player passes. What is your response?

1. ♠ K Q 8
   ♡ A J 7
   ◇ K 9 7 2
   ♣ 8 4 3

2. ♠ K Q 8
   ♡ A J 7
   ◇ K 9 7 2
   ♣ A 8 4

3. ♠ 8 7 4
   ♡ A J 7
   ◇ K 9 7 2
   ♣ A Q 3

4. ♠ K Q 8
   ♡ A J 7 4 2
   ◇ K 9
   ♣ J 8 3

5. ♠ A J 8 2
   ♡ A J 7 6
   ◇ A Q 7 4
   ♣ 7

6. ♠ A J 8 2
   ♡ A J 7 6
   ◇ 7
   ♣ A Q 7 4

7. ♠ A J 8 2
   ♡ 7
   ◇ A Q 7 4
   ♣ A J 7 6

8. ♠ 7 6
   ♡ A Q J 4
   ◇ A K 9
   ♣ A Q 3 2

B. Partner opens 1◇, next player passes. What is your response?

1. ♠ A 7
   ♡ A 9 7
   ◇ Q J 8 4 3
   ♣ 9 4 2

2. ♠ A 7
   ♡ A 9 7 2
   ◇ Q J 8 4 3
   ♣ K 6

3. ♠ K Q 8 4
   ♡ K 8 7 2
   ◇ 9 3
   ♣ K 6 5

4. ♠ A Q 8 4 3
   ♡ K Q 7 3 2
   ◇ K 3
   ♣ 5

5. ♠ A K Q J 7
   ♡ A 9
   ◇ Q J 8 4
   ♣ 9 4

6. ♠ A 7 6 3 2
   ♡ A 9
   ◇ Q J 8 4
   ♣ A K

7. ♠ 7 2
   ♡ A 9
   ◇ Q J 8 4 3
   ♣ A Q J 2

8. ♠ 7 3 2
   ♡ A K 9 7
   ◇ 3
   ♣ A K J 4 2

C. Partner opens 1♡, next player passes. What is your response?

1. ♠ A Q 9 8
   ♡ K Q 7 2
   ◇ K 3
   ♣ 7 6 3

2. ♠ A Q 9 8
   ♡ K 7 2
   ◇ K Q 3 2
   ♣ 7 6

3. ♠ 8 4 3
   ♡ K 3
   ◇ Q J 7 6
   ♣ A J 9 8

4. ♠ 8 4
   ♡ 3
   ◇ A Q 9 7 6
   ♣ A K 8 4 3

D. Partner opens 1♠, next player passes. What is your response?

1. ♠ A J 7
   ♡ 6 4 2
   ◇ K Q 9 3
   ♣ J 8 7

2. ♠ A J 7
   ♡ K Q 9 3 2
   ◇ K 7
   ♣ 8 4 2

3. ♠ 7 4
   ♡ A Q 8 6
   ◇ A K 9 3
   ♣ 8 4 2

4. ♠ Q 8 4 3
   ♡ K 8
   ◇ A J 6 3
   ♣ J 6 2

E. Partner opens 1NT, next player passes. What is your response?

1. ♠ K Q 8 7 6
   ♡ A 8
   ◇ J 6 3 2
   ♣ K 8

2. ♠ A 7
   ♡ K 8 3
   ◇ J 9 8 7 3 2
   ♣ A 6

3. ♠ - - -
   ♡ J 9 8 7 6 3
   ◇ A K Q 2
   ♣ J 6 5

4. ♠ 4
   ♡ K Q 9 5 3
   ◇ A Q J 6 4
   ♣ A K

OPENER'S REBIDS AFTER A STRONG RESPONSE

After a jump-raise of a major
Pass with minimum points and 5-3-3-2 shape. With 14 points or more or with a hand that is not balanced, bid on to at least game.

After a jump-raise of a minor
Pass if minimum. With a balanced hand, opener will be strong enough to try for 3NT (otherwise the opening bid would have been 1NT). With 14 HCP or more and not a balanced hand, opener is also worth a try for game.

After a jump to 2NT
Stay with no-trumps with a balanced hand, but aim for a trump contract if the hand is unbalanced. For example, after 1♠ : 2NT, opener could rebid 3♡ to show five spades and four hearts and a desire to play in one of the majors.

After a jump to 3NT
Responder's strength and hand pattern is known. Opener should judge whether to stay with no-trumps or whether to choose a suit contract.

After any of the above, opener will usually pass or try for game but with a very powerful hand, opener should explore slam prospects (see Chapter 8).

After a suit response at the 1-level
A suit response at the 1-level can be a weak responding hand or a strong responding hand. Opener's rebids have been discussed on pages 49-52.

After a jump-shift response
Opener should support responder's suit with three or more trumps. Without support, make a natural rebid, bidding a second suit if possible.

After a suit response at the 2-level (e.g., 1♡ : 2♣)

With a minimum opening, your order of priorities are :

● Support responder to the 3-level (e.g., 1♡ : 2♣, 3♣). Opener would choose not to support responder at once only after 1♠ : 2♣ or 1♠ : 2◊, where opener with four hearts would rather bid 2♡ to show the other major.

● Bid a new suit lower-ranking than the first suit (e.g., 1♡ : 2♣, 2◊). The change of suit to a lower suit has a range of 12-18 points, since a jump-shift needs 19 points or more. It may be a minimum opening or a strong opening, and therefore change-of-suit after a 2-level response is forcing.

● Repeat the first suit with at least 5 cards in the suit (e.g., 1♡ : 2♣, 2♡).

With a stronger hand which is balanced, rebid 2NT if 15-16 points and 3NT if 17-19. If the hand is not balanced, a new suit by opener beyond 2-in-the-suit-opened (e.g., 1◊ : 2♣, 2♡) shows better than a minimum opening, usually 16 points or more. Logically it is forcing to game since responder has 10 points or more for the 2-level response and opener has shown 16 points or more for a strong rebid.

REBIDDING AFTER A TWO-OVER-ONE SUIT RESPONSE
N.B. Opener must not pass. Describe your hand as best you can.
(L = Limit Bid, W-R = Wide-range, S-O = Sign-off, F = forcing, NF = Not forcing)

TYPE OF ACTION	SAMPLE AUCTION	SHOWING	FORCING?
Raise Responder Simple raise	1♥ : 2♣ 3♣	L : Minimum hand (12-15) and 4-card support	Not forcing
	1♠ : 2♥ 3♥	L : As 2♥ = 5+ suit, support can be 3 trumps	Not forcing
Jump-raise	1♥ : 2♣ 4♣	Strong hand, 16+ points, excellent 4+ support	Forcing to game
Game raise	1♠ : 2♥ 4♥	Strong hand, enough for game opposite 10 points	NF but consider slam prospects
Bid a new suit At the two-level (i) Lower-ranking	1♥ : 2♣ 2♦	W-R, 12-18 points at least 5-4 in the suits bid	Forcing for one round
(ii) Higher-ranking	1♥ : 2♣ 2♠	16+ points, first suit is 5+ and longer than second	Forcing to game
At the three-level	1♠ : 2♥ 3♦	16+ points, at least 5-4 in the suits bid	Forcing to game
Jump-shift	1♥ : 2♣ 3♦	Super hand, 19+ points, 5+ cards in the suits bid	Forcing to game
Bid no-trumps 2NT	1♥ : 2♣ 2NT	L : 15-16 points, balanced, opener's major may be 5	Not forcing
3NT	1♥ : 2♣ 3NT	L : 17-19 points, balanced	Not forcing
Rebid own suit Cheapest rebid	1♥ : 2♣ 2♥	L : Minimum hand, 12-15, and 5+ suit	Not forcing
Jump-rebid	1♥ : 2♣ 3♥	L : Strong hand, 16-18, plus good 6+ suit	Forcing to game
Game rebid	1♥ : 2♣ 4♥	Strong hand, 16+ points and self-sufficient suit	NF but consider slam prospects

EXERCISES ON REBIDS AFTER A STRONG RESPONSE

A. West 1◇ : East 2NT. West's rebid?

1. ♠ K 7	2. ♠ K 7	3. ♠ 6	4. ♠ A 7
♡ 8 4 3	♡ K Q 4	♡ 5 4	♡ 6 5
◇ A Q 6 5 4	◇ A K J 6 2	◇ A K J 8 6	◇ K Q 9 8 2
♣ A Q 2	♣ 9 4 2	♣ A Q J 6 3	♣ A J 4 3

B. West 1◇ : East 2♣. West's rebid?

1. ♠ K Q 3	2. ♠ K Q 3	3. ♠ K 3 2	4. ♠ K 3 2
♡ A K 7	♡ A 8 7	♡ A Q 8 6	♡ A Q 8 6
◇ K J 7 4	◇ K Q J 4	◇ K J 9 8 7	◇ A K J 7 4
♣ 8 6 2	♣ A 10 7	♣ 4	♣ 2

5. ♠ 7 2	6. ♠ 3	7. ♠ Q 3	8. ♠ Q 3
♡ A 2	♡ A K	♡ A K 7	♡ A K 7 6
◇ A Q 8 7 4	◇ A Q 8 7 4	◇ A K J 7 4 3	◇ A K J 7 4 3
♣ K 4 3 2	♣ K 9 8 6 2	♣ 6 2	♣ 2

C. West 1♡ : East 2♣. West's rebid?

1. ♠ A 4	2. ♠ A 9 8 3	3. ♠ 9 7 5	4. ♠ J 8
♡ K Q 7 6 2	♡ K Q 7 6 2	♡ A K J 7 3	♡ A Q 7 4 2
◇ A 9 8 3	◇ 7 6	◇ 9 7 2	◇ K Q
♣ 7 6	♣ A 4	♣ A 10	♣ J 8 6 2

5. ♠ K J 8	6. ♠ A J 8 2	7. ♠ A J 8	8. ♠ 7 2
♡ A Q 7 6 4	♡ A Q 6 3 2	♡ A Q J 9 4 2	♡ A 9 7 3 2
◇ K 7 4	◇ K Q	◇ A 4 2	◇ A K Q 5 4
♣ K 2	♣ K 2	♣ 3	♣ A

D. West 1♡ : East 2NT. West's rebid?

1. ♠ J 9 7	2. ♠ A J 7	3. ♠ A 6	4. ♠ - - -
♡ K J 9 5 4	♡ K J 9 8 4 3	♡ A 9 7 5 3	♡ A Q 8 7 5
◇ 7	◇ 7	◇ K 8 3	◇ K Q 7 6 3
♣ A K J 3	♣ K Q 2	♣ J 6 2	♣ Q J 8

E. West 1♠ : East 2◇. West's rebid?

1. ♠ A K 9 8 3	2. ♠ A K 9 8 3	3. ♠ A K J 7 3 2	4. ♠ A Q J 9 8 6 3
♡ K Q 7 6	♡ 8 5 3	♡ A 4 3	♡ 7 2
◇ 4	◇ 4	◇ 9 2	◇ K Q J
♣ 8 5 3	♣ K Q 7 6	♣ K Q	♣ J

PARTNERSHIP BIDDING PRACTICE
FEATURING RESPONDING WITH STRONG HANDS

West is the dealer on each hand. How should the bidding go?

WEST	EAST	WEST	EAST
23. ♠ A J 9 7	23. ♠ 8 2	30. ♠ A J 8	30. ♠ K Q 10
♡ K Q 4	♡ A J 7 2	♡ K Q J 8 7 2	♡ 9 5
◊ 7 6	◊ K 9 4 3	◊ K 9 4	◊ Q 8 5 3
♣ A J 3 2	♣ K Q 6	♣ 7	♣ A 8 4 2
24. ♠ A Q J 7 3	24. ♠ 8 2	31. ♠ A 7	31. ♠ 9 4 3
♡ 4	♡ A J 7 2	♡ 7 2	♡ K J 8 4
◊ 7	◊ K 9 4 3	◊ K Q J 5 3	◊ A 7
♣ A J 9 5 4 3	♣ K Q 6	♣ A Q 10 6	♣ K 5 3 2
25. ♠ A K J	25. ♠ 9 5	32. ♠ A 10 6	32. ♠ K 5
♡ K 7	♡ Q 10 6 5 2	♡ K 8 4 3	♡ Q J 6 5
◊ 7 2	◊ A K J 9	◊ K Q 9 6 2	◊ 8 7
♣ A J 9 8 4 3	♣ 6 2	♣ 8	♣ A K 9 4 3
26. ♠ J 6	26. ♠ 9 5	33. ♠ A 6	33. ♠ 7 2
♡ K J 3	♡ Q 10 6 5 2	♡ 4 3	♡ K Q J 8 5 2
◊ Q 7	◊ A K J 9	◊ A Q 8 7 4	◊ 6 2
♣ A J 9 8 4 3	♣ K 2	♣ K Q J 3	♣ A 5 2
27. ♠ 7 6 4 3	27. ♠ Q 2	34. ♠ K Q 6	34. ♠ A 8 4 3
♡ A Q 8 7	♡ K J 4 2	♡ 7 2	♡ A 10 5 3
◊ 6	◊ A K 9 7 5	◊ A Q 9 7 5 3	◊ K 4
♣ A K 4 3	♣ 8 6	♣ J 8	♣ K 9 2
28. ♠ Q J 3	28. ♠ K 4	35. ♠ 7	35. ♠ A K J 3
♡ A Q 8 7	♡ 6 2	♡ J 2	♡ K Q 9 4
◊ 6	◊ A K J 8 7 5	◊ A J 7 6 2	◊ 9 3
♣ A K 5 4 3	♣ 9 7 2	♣ A Q 9 7 5	♣ J 6 2
29. ♠ Q J 3	29. ♠ K 9 2	36. ♠ Q J 3 2	36. ♠ K 10 7 4
♡ 8 7	♡ A Q 2	♡ 9	♡ K Q J 7
◊ A Q 6 2	◊ K 8 7 4 3	◊ A Q 6 4	◊ 9 7
♣ A K 5 4	♣ 3 2	♣ A K 9 7	♣ Q 6 5

PARTNERSHIP BIDDING PRACTICE
FEATURING RESPONDING WITH STRONG HANDS

West is the dealer on each hand. How should the bidding go?

WEST	EAST	WEST	EAST
37. ♠ 8 6 5 3	37. ♠ A K 9 4 2	44. ♠ A K J 8 7	44. ♠ Q 5 4
♥ A J 7 4 3	♥ 6	♥ A Q J 6 3	♥ 8 2
♦ A K	♦ Q 8 3	♦ 7 3	♦ A K J 6 2
♣ 8 2	♣ Q J 10 5	♣ 8	♣ K 7 2
38. ♠ 8	38. ♠ A K 9 4 2	45. ♠ A K J 8 7	45. ♠ 6
♥ A Q 7 4 3 2	♥ 6	♥ A Q J 6 3	♥ K 8 4 2
♦ A K 9	♦ Q J 3	♦ 7 3	♦ A Q 8 6 4
♣ 8 6 2	♣ Q J 10 5	♣ 8	♣ Q 9 7
39. ♠ A J 9	39. ♠ Q 8 2	46. ♠ A K J 8 7	46. ♠ 9 6
♥ K Q 9 4 3	♥ J 5	♥ A Q J 6	♥ K 8
♦ A 10 4 2	♦ J 8 7	♦ 7 3	♦ A Q 8 6 4
♣ 6	♣ A K 8 7 3	♣ 8 5	♣ Q 9 7 2
40. ♠ K 9 5 2	40. ♠ 8 6 3	47. ♠ K Q 6 5 4	47. ♠ 8
♥ A K J 8 7	♥ Q	♥ A 2	♥ K Q 8 7 6 3
♦ Q 3 2	♦ A 6 5	♦ A Q 9 8 3	♦ K J 6
♣ K	♣ A Q 8 6 5 2	♣ Q	♣ J 7 2
41. ♠ A K J 2	41. ♠ Q 7 6 5 4	48. ♠ A Q 8 7 4	48. ♠ J 6
♥ K 9 7 6 4	♥ 5 3	♥ J 6	♥ A 8 7 4 3
♦ A 2	♦ K J 9 4 3	♦ K Q J	♦ A 9 5
♣ 6 3	♣ 4	♣ 9 8 3	♣ J 4 2
42. ♠ 6	42. ♠ J 8 7	49. ♠ A Q 8 7 4	49. ♠ J 6
♥ A Q 9 7 6	♥ 8 3	♥ J 6 2	♥ A K 8 4 3
♦ K Q J 5	♦ A 9 8 3 2	♦ K Q J	♦ A 9 5
♣ 9 3 2	♣ A J 4	♣ 9 8	♣ J 6 4
43. ♠ 6	43. ♠ J 8 7	50. ♠ Q J 7 6 2	50. ♠ K 3
♥ A Q 9 7 6	♥ K 8 3	♥ A Q 8 2	♥ K J 7 5
♦ K Q J 5	♦ A 9 8 3 2	♦ 6	♦ Q J 7 5
♣ 9 3 2	♣ A J	♣ A K 5	♣ 6 4 3

TIPS ON DECLARER PLAY

For maximum benefit, take a pack of cards, set out the cards below and follow the play as described.

Locating the missing cards

NORTH
Dummy
♠ 8 7 6 4 3

SOUTH
♠ A K J 10

How should you play this combination? With nine cards missing the queen, the best chance is to play the ace and king and hope that the queen falls. This is known as playing for the drop. As only four cards are missing, there is a good chance that the queen will be singleton or doubleton.

Suppose when you play the ace, your left-hand opponent (West) shows out. You know that the suit has divided 4-0 and that all the missing cards are with East. If you continue with the king, East's queen will win a trick.

As you hold the jack and ten, you are able to capture East's queen if you play the cards in correct order. After the ace reveals that West is void, cross to the North hand in some other suit. Then lead a low spade and watch what East plays. If it is the queen, you will capture it, of course. If it is a low card, you can play the jack (or ten) and win the trick since you know that West is void. The technical name for this play is a 'finesse'. We say that you have 'finessed the jack'.

A finesse is attempting to win a trick with a card lower than a card held by the opponents. Your jack is lower than their queen. In this case you know that the finesse is sure to succeed. Such a finesse is called a 'marked finesse'.

After winning with the jack you know that East still has Q-x left. It still does you no good to cash your king. East's queen will then be high. The winning move is to return to the North hand once more in some other suit and again lead a low spade. This forces East to play second to the trick. If East plays a low spade, you will finesse the ten. Then your king captures East's queen.

The technique is to force the player known to have the missing card to play second on the trick. This called 'leading through' that player. Your move depends on which card the second player has produced. If it is the missing honour, you capture it. If not, you can finesse against it.

NORTH
Dummy
♦ A K Q 10

SOUTH
♦ 7 6 3 2

You start by playing the ace and king. On the second round, East on your right shows out. You know that five cards were missing originally. East started with just one and so West began with four to the jack. West still has J-x left. You must not play your queen. That makes the jack high. Instead come to your hand and lead low through West. If West plays low, finesse the ten.

PLAY HANDS ON STRONG RESPONDING HANDS

(These hands can be made up by using pages 157-160)

Hand 13 : Coping with a bad break — The marked finesse

Dealer North : Nil vulnerable

NORTH
♠ 10 7 4
♡ A K Q 10
◇ K
♣ J 8 7 6 2

WEST
♠ A K 8 6 3
♡ J 9 8 2
◇ A 9
♣ Q 9

EAST
♠ 9 5 2
♡ - - -
◇ 10 8 7 6 5 4
♣ 10 5 4 3

SOUTH
♠ Q J
♡ 7 6 5 4 3
◇ Q J 3 2
♣ A K

WEST	NORTH	EAST	SOUTH
	1♣	Pass	1♡
1♠	2♡	Pass	4♡
Pass	Pass	Pass	

Bidding : With 13 points opposite an opening, South always intended to reach game. When North raised hearts, that settled the matter.

Lead : ♠A, normal from A-K suits.

Play : After the top spades and the ◇A, win the next trick and play the ♡A. When East shows out, play a club to hand and lead a heart towards dummy, *finessing* the 10 when West plays low. Draw West's trumps and use the ♠10 or the ♣J to discard a diamond loser.

Hand 14 : Drawing trumps — The marked finesse

Dealer East : N-S vulnerable

NORTH
♠ - - -
♡ J 10 5 4
◇ A 7 5 3
♣ 8 7 4 3 2

WEST
♠ A K J 5
♡ 8 7 3 2
◇ Q 9 4
♣ J 6

EAST
♠ 9 7 6 4 3 2
♡ A K Q
◇ K J
♣ Q 9

SOUTH
♠ Q 10 8
♡ 9 6
◇ 10 8 6 2
♣ A K 10 5

WEST	NORTH	EAST	SOUTH
		1♠	Pass
3♠	Pass	4♠	All pass

Bidding : West's 3♠ jump-raise shows 10-12 points and 4+ support. East has enough extra to bid to game.

Lead : ♣A, normal from A-K suits.

Play : South switches to a red suit after cashing the top clubs. When East comes in, East leads a spade to the ace. When North shows out, East knows South began with Q-10-8 and still has Q-x left. To capture the queen, East returns to hand with a heart and leads a spade, finessing dummy's jack and drawing the last trump. East loses just three tricks.

Hand 15 : Drawing trumps in the correct order — The marked finesse

Dealer South : Both vulnerable

NORTH
- ♠ A 9 7 5
- ♥ K Q 4 2
- ♦ 8 5 2
- ♣ K Q

WEST
- ♠ Q J 4
- ♥ 9
- ♦ A K Q 10 7
- ♣ 8 6 4 2

EAST
- ♠ 10 8 6 3 2
- ♥ J 8 6 5
- ♦ 9 4
- ♣ 7 5

SOUTH
- ♠ K
- ♥ A 10 7 3
- ♦ J 6 3
- ♣ A J 10 9 3

WEST	NORTH	EAST	SOUTH
			1♣
1♦	1♥	Pass	2♥
Pass	4♥	All pass	

Bidding : 1♥ was up-the-line.

Lead : ♦9. Partner's suit is first choice. High-low with a doubleton.

Play : After three diamond tricks and a black suit exit, play off the K-Q of hearts first (keep the A-10 tenace intact). When West discards, finesse against East's jack, thus not losing a heart trick. If trumps were 3-2, the order of playing the top trumps would not matter. K-Q first caters for East holding J-x-x-x. Had West continued with a fourth diamond, a careful North would ruff this in hand.

Hand 16 : Drawing trumps — Marked finesse — Repeating the finesse

Dealer West : Nil vulnerable

NORTH
- ♠ - - -
- ♥ 10 9 6 3 2
- ♦ 9 7 5 4 2
- ♣ A K 8

WEST
- ♠ A J 10 7 4 3
- ♥ K 8 4
- ♦ A 10
- ♣ 6 3

EAST
- ♠ K 5 2
- ♥ Q J 7
- ♦ K Q J
- ♣ J 9 4 2

SOUTH
- ♠ Q 9 8 6
- ♥ A 5
- ♦ 8 6 3
- ♣ Q 10 7 5

WEST	NORTH	EAST	SOUTH
1♠	Pass	3NT	Pass
4♠	Pass	Pass	Pass

Bidding : After 3NT (a 4-3-3-3 with a 4-card minor) West removes to 4♠.

Lead : ♣A, normal from A-K suits.

Play : South plays the ♣7 on the ace and the ♣5 on the king. High-low on partner's lead is a signal for partner to continue that suit. West ruffs the next club and leads a spade to the king, high card from shortage. When North shows out, West continues by finessing the jack of spades, leading a diamond to dummy and finessing the ♠10. The ♠A draws South's queen and declarer then sets up the winners in hearts.

CHAPTER 6

BIDDING BY A PASSED HAND

Once you have passed initially, the meaning of some of your bids will be affected. A passed hand cannot hold 12 HCP. With that, you would have opened the bidding.

The weak responses are not affected : a raise of opener's suit to the two-level is still 6-9 points and so is the 1NT response. Likewise, the jump to 2NT has its usual meaning (11-12 points, balanced shape, stoppers in the unbid suits) and the jump-raise of opener's suit is still 10-12 points with at least four trumps. Here you might have 12 points or more, since with support you can add on your Ruffing Points (5 for a void, 3 for a singleton and 1 for a doubleton).

A change of suit at the one-level has a range of 6-12 points. This contrasts with the unlimited nature of the 6 *or more* points attached to the response of a new suit by an unpassed hand. Similarly, the change of suit to the 2-level has a narrow 10-11 point range. By an unpassed hand, the change of suit to the 2-level is 10 points *or more*. Note that even as a passed hand, a response at the 2-level promises 10 points.

A jump-shift by a passed hand (e.g., Pass : 1◊, 2♠) shows exactly 10-11 points. It also promises a strong 5-card suit. If the suit has only four cards or if the suit is not strong, bid the suit at the cheapest level without a jump.

The most important rule about bidding by a passed hand is this :

A BID BY A PASSED HAND IS NOT FORCING.

This applies whether it is a jump-bid or a change of suit so that the normal rules about change-of-suit forcing or jump-responses in a new suit forcing to game and suggesting slam do not apply when the responder is a passed hand. Because any bid by a passed hand is not forcing, it is vital to make a response which gives partner the most important message in one bid. There might be no second chance. Therefore, raise a major suit as first priority. Do not bid a new suit when you have a major suit raise available.

EXERCISES ON PASSED HAND BIDDING

A. You passed as dealer and partner opens 1♣. What is your response?

1. ♠ K Q 6	2. ♠ A J	3. ♠ A Q J 4 3	4. ♠ K 8
♡ K J 8	♡ K Q 3 2	♡ K 9	♡ A Q 9
◊ Q 10 5 2	◊ J 7 6	◊ 7 6 5	◊ 6 3
♣ 10 9 2	♣ 8 7 4 2	♣ J 9 2	♣ J 8 7 5 3 2

B. You passed as dealer and partner opens 1♡. What is your response?

1. ♠ A J	2. ♠ A J 8 4 2	3. ♠ K Q 6	4. ♠ A Q J 9 8
♡ K 9 7 6	♡ Q 7 6 2	♡ 4 3	♡ J 6
◊ 6 5 4	◊ 4 3	◊ J 10 4 3	◊ K 4 3
♣ Q J 9 4	♣ 6 2	♣ A J 10 2	♣ 7 6 2

5. ♠ A 9 8 6	6. ♠ A 5 2	7. ♠ A 5 2	8. ♠ 5 2
♡ 7	♡ 4 3	♡ 4	♡ 7 6 4 3
◊ Q 9 8 4	◊ K J 9 8 2	◊ K J 8 2	◊ A K J 8
♣ K J 8 2	♣ Q 4 2	♣ 9 7 5 4 3	♣ Q J 2

PARTNERSHIP BIDDING PRACTICE

West is the dealer on each hand. How should the bidding go?

WEST	EAST	WEST	EAST
51. ♠ A J 7	51. ♠ 9 5	54. ♠ A 7 6 4 2	54. ♠ J 9 8
♡ K 9 8 4	♡ A Q 6 3 2	♡ K J	♡ 10 4 3
◊ 7 6 4 3 2	◊ A K 8	◊ Q 9 8	◊ J 5
♣ 6	♣ J 7 4	♣ J 6 2	♣ A K Q 9 3
52. ♠ A Q 7 2	52. ♠ K 9 4 3	55. ♠ A J 7	55. ♠ Q 3 2
♡ K 9 8 3	♡ 7	♡ 8 7	♡ K Q 6 3 2
◊ J 8 7	◊ A K 3	◊ K 8 2	◊ A 7
♣ 4 2	♣ A J 9 5 3	♣ K 8 6 4 3	♣ A 9 7
53. ♠ Q 7	53. ♠ K 9 8 5 2	56. ♠ 7	56. ♠ Q J 6 4 3
♡ A 8	♡ K 7 6	♡ A 9 8 2	♡ Q 7
◊ Q J 8 6 4 3	◊ 9 5 2	◊ J 9 7 3	◊ A 8 5
♣ 7 6 2	♣ A Q	♣ A Q 7 6	♣ K 5 2

CHAPTER 7

OPENING WITH A TWO-BID

Hands with more than 21 HCP are too strong to open with a one-opening, since partner will normally pass with 5 points or less.

♠ A K J 8 4 3   If you were to open this hand with 1♠, imagine your
♡ A K 3   dismay if the bidding went : Pass, Pass, Pass. With just
◊ A K Q   two or three points, partner would be quite right to pass
♣ 5   but game may be a great chance opposite even less.

To cope with such powerhouses, open with a Two-Bid.

2NT = 20-22 HCP and balanced shape. Partner may pass this with 0-3 points but with any more, partner will respond as the partnership could have 26 points. With a balanced hand, responder keeps to no-trumps, while with unbalanced shapes, bid three-in-a-suit (promises a 5-card suit and is forcing) or bid game in a major suit with six cards or more in the major. The Stayman 3♣ Convention is also commonly used in response to 2NT (see Appendix 1).

The 2♣ Opening

Any hand with 23 HCP or more should be opened 2♣. Except for one sequence the 2♣ opening is forcing to game. You may also open 2♣ with less than 23 HCP if your hand has at least ten playing tricks.

How to count playing tricks : *In your long suits (four or more cards) :* Count the ace and king as winners. Count the queen as a winner if the suit contains another honour. Count every card after the third card as a winner.
In your short suits : Count A = 1, K with another honour = 1, K with one or more cards but no other honour = ½, Q or J with at least one higher honour = ½ (but A-K-Q is of course three tricks).

Opening 2◊, 2♡ or 2♠

These show a long, strong suit with at least eight playing tricks and are forcing for one round. Hands with such a long suit and 21 points or more (counting HCP plus Length Points) are also suitable for these openings.

♠ A K Q J 7 6 3   This hand is worth nine tricks with spades as
♡ K Q J   trumps. It would be a tragedy to open 1♠ and be
◊ 6   left there. Open 2♠ and rebid 3♠. To open 3♠ or
♣ 6 2   4♠ has a different meaning — see Chapter 9.

RESPONDING TO 2♣

While responder is expected to pass a one-opening with 0-5 points, *responder must reply to a 2♣ opening,* no matter how weak the hand.

Responder's weakness reply to 2♣ is 2◊ : 0-7 HCP and any shape.
Any other reply is a positive answer with 8 or more points, about 1½ quick tricks or better. A positive response often leads to a slam. The quick trick count is A-K = 2, A-Q = 1½, A = 1, K-Q = 1 and K = ½.

The 2♣ opening is artificial and so is the 2◊ negative response. 7 points is borderline for the 2◊ reply. An ace plus a king is worth a positive response and so is a hand including a 5-card or longer suit headed by the A-Q.

If there happens to be an intervening bid over partner's 2♣ opening, responder would pass to show the negative reply. There is no obligation to bid over an intervening bid, since opener has another chance to bid anyway.

After a positive response

Bidding proceeds naturally, with the partnership endeavouring to establish a trump fit. The normal rules apply for bidding suits : longest first; with a 5-5 or 6-6, bid the higher suit first; 4-card suits up-the-line. With a balanced hand, responder bids 2NT with 8 HCP or more. The 2♣ : 2NT, 3NT sequence shows opener has a balanced hand of 23-24 points and wishes to leave slam bidding up to responder.

Responder is entitled to expect the first genuine suit bid by opener to be a 5-card or longer suit and may therefore support it with just three trumps. If opener repeats the first suit, responder may support it with a doubleton. A second suit may be just four cards and so four trumps are needed to support opener's second suit.

AFTER 2♣ : 2◊

2♣ : 2◊, 2NT

The 2NT rebid shows opener has a balanced hand of 23-24 points. This rebid is not forcing, but responder with 2 points or more will bid on to game. Bidding after this 2NT *rebid* is the same as bidding after a 2NT *opening*.

Any rebid by opener other than 2NT is forcing to game. Neither opener nor responder should pass until at least game is reached. Bidding proceeds along natural lines. Responder will strive to support opener. If that is not possible, responder may introduce a long suit or rebid in no-trumps.

Bidding after 2◊, 2♡ or 2♠

The negative reply is 2NT. Any other reply is natural and commits the partnership to game. The requirements for a positive response are the same as after 2♣ and suits are shown in the normal order. After the negative reply, opener's rebid of the suit opened is not forcing but responder should bid with 5-7 points. A new suit rebid by opener is forcing for one round.

EXERCISES ON SUPER-STRONG OPENING BIDS

A. What is your opening bid on these hands?

1.	♠ A 6	2.	♠ A	3.	♠ A K Q 8 4 3
	♡ A K Q 10 6 2		♡ A K Q		♡ A K J 9 8
	◊ A K		◊ A K J 10 6 5 2		◊ 5
	♣ 9 7 3		♣ 5 3		♣ 4

4.	♠ Q 7 5 4 3	5.	♠ - - -	6.	♠ A K Q J
	♡ A K 6 5 2		♡ A K Q 8 6 5 4		♡ A Q J 7
	◊ A K		◊ A Q J 8 7 3		◊ 4
	♣ A		♣ - - -		♣ A K Q 8

B. Partner opens 2♣, next player passes. What is your response?

1.	♠ 7 5 4	2.	♠ K 8 7	3.	♠ A 8 7	4.	♠ A 8 7
	♡ 6 4 2		♡ 6 4		♡ 6 4		♡ 4 2
	◊ 5 4 3 2		◊ K 6 5 3		◊ Q J 7 6		◊ K Q 5 3 2
	♣ 7 6 3		♣ 9 8 6 4		♣ Q 9 6 2		♣ 9 8 4

5.	♠ A J 7 4	6.	♠ A 9 8 4	7.	♠ 7 6	8.	♠ A K 2
	♡ K Q 9 8		♡ K 7 5 3 2		♡ 7 5		♡ 8 7 2
	◊ 7 4 3 2		◊ 4 2		◊ A Q J 8 7 6		◊ A J 7 5
	♣ 6		♣ 8 6		♣ 8 5 4		♣ J 9 2

C. What would your answers be in Exercise B if partner had opened 2♡ ?

D. West 2♣ : East 2◊. West's rebid?

1.	♠ A K Q J 7	2.	♠ A K Q J 8 7 6	3.	♠ A Q J 8
	♡ A K J 4		♡ 5 3		♡ 6
	◊ 4 3		◊ A 4		◊ A K J 10
	♣ A K		♣ A K		♣ A K Q 5

4.	♠ A K Q 8	5.	♠ A Q J	6.	♠ A K Q
	♡ K J 5		♡ A K Q		♡ 6 4 3
	◊ A K 10 3		◊ K Q J 5		◊ A K Q
	♣ K 3		♣ A J 7		♣ A Q 7 2

7.	♠ A 7	8.	♠ A K Q 7	9.	♠ A K 7
	♡ 4		♡ A Q		♡ 8
	◊ A K Q 4 3		◊ 4		◊ K Q
	♣ A K Q 7 6		♣ A K J 10 8 3		♣ A K Q J 6 3 2

E. West 2♠ : East 2NT, West rebids 3♡. What should East rebid?

1. ♠ 6 5
   ♡ 4 3
   ◇ Q J 6 5
   ♣ 8 7 6 4 2

2. ♠ 9 8 7
   ♡ 7 6
   ◇ Q J 7 6 3
   ♣ 4 3 2

3. ♠ Q 8 7
   ♡ 4
   ◇ 8 7 5 3 2
   ♣ K 9 6 5

4. ♠ 8
   ♡ 7 2
   ◇ A J 8 6 5 3 2
   ♣ 5 3 2

5. ♠ 6 5
   ♡ 7 6 4 3
   ◇ 9 6 5 3 2
   ♣ 9 8

6. ♠ J 8 7
   ♡ J 5 2
   ◇ J 5 4 2
   ♣ 5 3 2

7. ♠ 3 2
   ♡ 9
   ◇ Q J 8 7 6
   ♣ Q J 9 8 2

8. ♠ - - -
   ♡ 9 4 3
   ◇ Q 7 6 3 2
   ♣ 9 7 5 3 2

F. West 2♡ : East 2NT, West rebids 6◇. What should East call now?

1. ♠ J 7 6 5 4
   ♡ 9 8 6
   ◇ 5 4
   ♣ 6 4 2

2. ♠ 6 4 3 2
   ♡ 4 3
   ◇ 8 7 5
   ♣ 5 4 3 2

3. ♠ 8 6 5 3
   ♡ 4
   ◇ K 7 5
   ♣ 9 6 5 3 2

4. ♠ 9 8 2
   ♡ A 7 6
   ◇ 4 3
   ♣ 7 6 5 3 2

PARTNERSHIP BIDDING PRACTICE

West is the dealer on each hand. How should the bidding go?

WEST	EAST	WEST	EAST
57. ♠ A K Q 9 ♡ Q 9 ◇ A K J 10 8 5 ♣ A	57. ♠ 6 4 3 ♡ J 8 6 3 2 ◇ 4 3 ♣ K 6 3	61. ♠ 7 ♡ A K 2 ◇ K Q J 10 8 6 ♣ A K 5	61. ♠ K J 9 8 5 ♡ 6 5 3 ◇ 2 ♣ J 10 7 6
58. ♠ Q 10 7 ♡ J 10 7 4 ◇ K 8 3 2 ♣ 7 2	58. ♠ A K 8 6 3 ♡ K ◇ - - - ♣ A Q J 9 8 5 4	62. ♠ 9 3 ♡ J 8 7 4 ◇ 6 3 ♣ Q 7 6 4 3	62. ♠ A K Q J 5 ♡ A K 6 2 ◇ A K ♣ K 2
59. ♠ A K J 9 8 3 ♡ A 6 ◇ 7 4 ♣ A K J	59. ♠ 5 4 2 ♡ J 10 4 ◇ J 5 2 ♣ 8 6 3 2	63. ♠ 6 4 ♡ Q 9 6 3 2 ◇ 8 6 3 ♣ 8 4 3	63. ♠ A 9 5 ♡ K J 5 ◇ A K Q ♣ K Q J 10
60. ♠ J 5 4 ♡ 9 7 ◇ Q 8 6 3 ♣ 9 8 5 3	60. ♠ A 9 ♡ A Q 2 ◇ A K 5 2 ♣ K Q J 6	64. ♠ K Q J 10 7 6 ♡ A ◇ - - - ♣ A K Q J 6 5	64. ♠ A 3 ♡ 6 5 4 2 ◇ 8 7 6 5 2 ♣ 4 3

TIPS ON DECLARER PLAY

Finessing

In the previous chapter we saw how to trap an enemy honour by finessing when we knew the location of the critical honour card. It is possible to do the same although you may not know which opponent holds that honour.

How many tricks do you have with this combination?

Dummy : A Q J

You :   7 6 3

You can score two tricks easily enough. Play the ace and then the queen to force out the king and make your jack high. That is two tricks for sure, but would it not be nice to win three tricks? You can do it if the layout of the suit is something like this, with the king with West :

```
                NORTH
                A Q J
      WEST                  EAST
      K 9 8 2               10 5 4

                SOUTH
                7 6 3
```

The A-Q-J combination is known as a tenace : you have a high card and a lower card and the opponents hold the card in between. To succeed with a finesse involving a tenace you must lead from the hand opposite the tenace. Here you lead a low card and force West to play before you commit yourself to playing from the tenace. If West plays the king you would capture it, of course, but that would be a foolish play by West. If West plays low, finesse the queen (or jack). If the king were with East, the finesse would lose. When the finesse wins, return to your own hand via some other suit and again lead towards your tenace. When West plays low again, finesse the jack. As long as West has the king, this play wins three tricks for you.

A K J 3	K J 10
5 4 2	6 3 2

To make the maximum number of tricks possible, cash the ace just in case the queen drops. If not, return to hand in another suit and lead low towards the K-J tenace. If West plays low, finesse the jack. If West has the queen, your jack will win the trick.

You have one trick for sure but to play for two tricks, lead from your hand and if West plays low, finesse dummy's jack. If this wins or forces out the ace, return to hand in another suit and again lead towards your K-10 tenace. If West plays low, finesse the 10.

PLAY HANDS ON OPENING TWO BIDS
(These hands can be made up by using pages 157-160)

Hand 17 : 2NT opening — Suit contract — Finessing

Dealer North : Nil vulnerable

WEST	NORTH	EAST	SOUTH
	2NT	Pass	4♡
Pass	Pass	Pass	

NORTH
♠ A Q J 3
♡ A K
◊ A 10 4 2
♣ Q J 9

WEST
♠ K 10 9
♡ 10
◊ 8 6 5 3
♣ A K 7 4 2

EAST
♠ 7 5 4
♡ 9 5 4 2
◊ K Q J 9
♣ 10 3

SOUTH
♠ 8 6 2
♡ Q J 8 7 6 3
◊ 7
♣ 8 6 5

Bidding : South knows N-S must have 8 or more hearts and has enough to bid game. Note that 3NT fails as there is no entry to the South hand.

Lead : ♣A, normal from A-K suits.

Play : East signals high-low, 10 then 3, in clubs, and ruffs the third round. The ◊A wins the ◊K exit and A-K of hearts are cashed. A diamond is ruffed and the last trump is drawn. A spade is led, finessing the queen. When this finesse succeeds, another diamond is ruffed and the jack of spades is finessed. Making 10 tricks.

Hand 18 : Demand opening — Weakness response — Finessing

Dealer East : N-S vulnerable

WEST	NORTH	EAST	SOUTH
		Pass	Pass
2♣	Pass	2◊	Pass
2♠	Pass	4♠	All pass

NORTH
♠ Q 10 9
♡ J 10 9 5 3
◊ 9 8
♣ A 8 7

WEST
♠ A K 7 5 2
♡ K Q
◊ A K J 6
♣ K Q

EAST
♠ J 8 6 4 3
♡ 8 7
◊ 5 4 3 2
♣ 5 3

SOUTH
♠ - - -
♡ A 6 4 2
◊ Q 10 7
♣ J 10 9 6 4 2

Bidding : 2◊ is the negative reply. West's 2♠ is forcing to game. 4♠ shows support and a very weak hand.

Lead : ♡J, top of sequence.

Play : When in, West plays A-K of spades. Normally leave the last trump out, but you need to reach dummy to take the diamond finesse. Concede a spade, win the return, cash one top diamond (in case the queen drops), cross to dummy with a trump and lead a diamond, finessing the jack. The finesse for a queen is normally taken on the second round of the suit.

Hand 19 : 2♣ : 2◇, 2NT sequence — Suit response — Finessing

Dealer South : N-S vulnerable

NORTH
♠ K
♡ 8 6 5 3 2
◇ 7 4 3 2
♣ 7 5 3

WEST
♠ J 10 5 3
♡ 9 4
◇ J 10 8
♣ 10 9 8 6

EAST
♠ 9 7 4 2
♡ K 10 7
◇ 9 6 5
♣ A K Q

SOUTH
♠ A Q 8 6
♡ A Q J
◇ A K Q
♣ J 4 2

WEST	NORTH	EAST	SOUTH
			2♣
Pass	2◇	Pass	2NT
Pass	3♡	Pass	4♡
Pass	Pass	Pass	

Bidding : The 2NT rebid = 23-24 points, balanced, and North's 3♡ shows *five* hearts. In 3NT, North's ♠K entry is easily knocked out.

Lead : ♣A, normal from A-K suits.

Play : East cashes three clubs and switches to a spade. North wins and the best chance to avoid a heart loser is to finesse for the king. Low heart, low, queen . . . the finesse works. Ruff a spade to come back to hand and lead a low heart, low, finesse the jack. The ♡A then captures the king.

Hand 20 : Refusing to overruff — Discarding a loser instead

Dealer West : Nil vulnerable

NORTH
♠ 9
♡ Q J 9 7 4
◇ K J 10 7 4
♣ 9 2

WEST
♠ 7 6
♡ K 8 5 2
◇ 9 8 6 3
♣ Q 10 7

EAST
♠ A K Q 8 4 3 2
♡ A 6
◇ A 2
♣ J 8

SOUTH
♠ J 10 5
♡ 10 3
◇ Q 5
♣ A K 6 5 4 3

WEST	NORTH	EAST	SOUTH
Pass	Pass	2♠	Pass
2NT	Pass	3♠	Pass
4♠	Pass	Pass	Pass

Bidding : 2♠ is forcing, but 3♠ is not. West has enough to bid 4♠.

Lead : ♣A, normal from A-K suits.

Play : North's high-low, 9 then 2 in clubs, asks South to continue clubs. North ruffs the third club with the ♠9. If East overruffs, South's J-10-5 becomes a trump trick and with a diamond to be lost, declarer is one down. This is unlucky for East but there is a safe counter-measure. On the third club, declarer should not overruff. Discard the ◇2 and ten tricks are quite safe.

CHAPTER 8

SLAM BIDDING

If you and partner have the values for a slam, it is a losing approach not to bid the slam. Even if you fail occasionally, the rewards for slams are so great that you will be in front in the long run if you succeed in more than 50% of your slams. A small slam is worthwhile with 33 points or more and a grand slam should be bid if you have at least 37 points together.

However, there is more to bidding slams than just points. It is also vital that you cannot lose the first two tricks in a small slam and that there should be little risk of a loser in a grand slam. In particular, there should not be two aces missing for a small slam, or an ace or a critical king or queen missing for a grand slam. The 33 points for a small slam need not all be high card points so that it is possible for two aces to be missing. Likewise, the 37 points for a grand slam can contain shortage points and again an ace or a key king or key queen could be missing. If you are in doubt, settle for a good small slam rather than take a risk for a grand slam.

If you know the partnership has 33 high card points or more, you know that there cannot be two aces missing. If you have located a good trump fit or you know that you should be in no-trumps, you can then simply bid the slam you judge to be best without further ado. For example, if partner opens 2NT and you hold 13 points with a 4-3-3-3 pattern, the commonsense bid is 6NT. You need no extra information to bid the slam. In other situations, you may know that there is enough strength for a slam and can tell that you cannot lose the first two tricks. For example :

♠ A 9 8 6 4 2   Partner passed, you opened 1♠ and partner raised to
♡ A Q   3♠. Since partner passed initially, you can expect the
♢ 5   jump-raise to show support and 11-12 total points.
♣ A K J 2   Your hand, now worth 22, is enough for a small slam.

As you hold three aces and a singleton in the other suit, there is no threat of losing the first two tricks. Bid 6♠.

Most of the time you may know that there are enough points for a slam, but two aces could be missing. There are two ways that you can deal with this problem. One is called cue-bidding where you show the aces that you hold, the other is the Blackwood Convention, asking for aces.

80

Cue-bidding

After the partnership has agreed on a trump suit and is committed to at least game, bidding a new suit says 'I am interested in slam and if this suit is led, I can win the trick.' Such a new suit bid is called a cue bid and shows first round control of the suit bid. First round control means that you can win the trick the first time that the suit is played. Either you have the ace in that suit, the common situation, or you are void in that suit and so can ruff if that suit is led.

WEST	EAST	
1♠	3♣	After 4♣ agreed the trump suit, 4◊, a new suit, is a cue bid and shows first round control in diamonds,
4♣	4◊	either the ace of diamonds or a void in diamonds.

When making a cue bid, bid the cheapest first round control. Had East bid 4♡ instead of 4◊, East would be saying 'I have control in hearts but not in diamonds.' By-passing 4◊ denies first round control in diamonds.

After partner has made a cue bid, bid the cheapest suit (excluding the trump suit) in which you also have first round control. If you have no outside ace or void, bid the agreed trump suit. In the above auction, if West bid 5♣ over 4◊, West would be saying 'I do not have the ace of hearts or the ace of spades' since West by-passed the 4♡ and 4♠ bids.

After first round controls have been shown, further cue bids show second round control in the suit bid. Second round control means that you can win the trick on the second round of that suit, either by means of the king or because you can ruff the second round (for example, you have a singleton).

WEST	EAST	
1♠	2♡	Hearts is the agreed the trump suit. 4♣ shows first
3♡	4♣	round control in clubs and slam interest. 4◊ = first
4◊	5♣	round diamond control. 5♣, a cue bid in a suit where a cue bid has already been made, = second round control in clubs, the king or a singleton or a void.

When a cue bid shows second round control it also says 'I have no other first round controls to show.' In the above auction, East would bid 4♠ over 4◊ with the ace of spades. By-passing 4♠ denies first round spade control.

Cue-bidding works well on slam-going hands where you have a void or where you hold a suit outside trumps which does not contain the ace or the king or a singleton.

WEST	EAST	WEST	EAST	
♠ A K Q J 8	♠ 9 7 6 3	2♣	2◊	4♣ = cue bid, showing first round club control
♡ - - -	♡ A 8 7 4	2♠	3♠	4♡ = cue bid, showing
◊ K Q J 9 5	◊ 6 4 3	4♣	4♡	first round heart control,
♣ A K Q	♣ J 2	6♠	Pass	denies diamond control

If East had the ace of diamonds, East would bid 4◊ over 4♣ and then West would bid 7♠. With no ace, East would bid 4♠ over 4♣.

The Blackwood Convention

The Blackwood Convention is a bid of 4NT, asking for aces. It works best on hands with no void and where each suit outside trumps contains the ace or the king or a singleton. Before you use 4NT, you should be confident that your side has the strength for a slam. Even all four aces and four kings add up to only eight tricks. In addition, you must know your final destination. You are sure that no-trumps is all right *or* you are aware of a strong trump fit *or* you have a powerful self-sufficient trump suit.

BLACKWOOD 4NT — ASKING FOR ACES

A BID OF 4NT AFTER A SUIT BID ASKS PARTNER :
'HOW MANY ACES DO YOU HAVE?'

THE REPLIES ARE :

$$5\clubsuit = 0 \text{ or } 4$$
$$5\diamondsuit = 1$$
$$5\heartsuit = 2$$
$$5\spadesuit = 3$$

AFTER THE ANSWER TO 4NT, 5NT ASKS PARTNER :
'HOW MANY KINGS DO YOU HOLD?'

THE REPLIES ARE :

$$6\clubsuit = 0$$
$$6\diamondsuit = 1$$
$$6\heartsuit = 2$$
$$6\spadesuit = 3$$
$$6NT = 4$$

To use the 5NT ask for kings, you should have ambitions for a grand slam. The partnership should have the values for a grand slam, a strong trump suit and there should not be any aces missing. In other words, the use of 5NT asking for kings promises that the partnership holds all the aces.

If 4NT is used as an immediate response to an opening bid of no-trumps (e.g., 1NT : 4NT or 2NT : 4NT) this is not used as Blackwood but as an invitation to 6NT. Opener is asked to pass with a minimum opening and to bid on with more than minimum points. If you wish to check on aces after an opening bid of no-trumps, you will need to bid a suit first (e.g., 1NT : 3♡ or 2NT : 3◊) and then bid 4NT later. It is an ask for aces if there has been a suit bid in the auction.

EXERCISES ON SLAM BIDDING

A. In each of the following auctions you are South with the hand shown. Would you say that you are in the slam zone or the game zone?

1. ♠ K 10 9 6 4
   ♥ K Q 5
   ◊ A 9 7 3
   ♣ 4

N	S
2NT	?

2. ♠ K 6 3
   ♥ K 9
   ◊ K 10 7 6 5 3
   ♣ A 2

N	S
2♥	?

3. ♠ K Q 7
   ♥ K J 4 3
   ◊ A 8 7
   ♣ A J 3

N	S
1NT	?

4. ♠ A K J
   ♥ Q J 7 4 3 2
   ◊ K Q
   ♣ J 6

N	S
	1♥
4♥	?

5. ♠ A Q
   ♥ A Q 8 4 3
   ◊ K 7 2
   ♣ Q 4 3

N	S
	1♥
3♥	?

6. ♠ 6
   ♥ K 9
   ◊ A J 3 2
   ♣ A K 9 7 6 2

N	S
1♥	2♣
3♥	?

B. What should South call next in each of these auctions?

1. ♠ A J 8 3
   ♥ A 6
   ◊ A Q J 4 2
   ♣ 8 3

N	S
	1◊
1♠	3♠
4NT	?

2. ♠ A 8 7
   ♥ A 4 3
   ◊ A J 10 4
   ♣ A K 4

N	S
	2NT
3♥	4♥
4NT	?

3. ♠ K Q
   ♥ K Q J 4 3
   ◊ 7 2
   ♣ A K 4 3

N	S
1♠	2♥
3♥	?

4. ♠ Q 4 3 2
   ♥ K 8 5
   ◊ 3
   ♣ A K J 6 4

N	S
1♥	2♣
2◊	4♥
4NT	?

5. ♠ K 8 4 2
   ♥ A 9
   ◊ Q J 9 8
   ♣ K 8 6

N	S
	1NT
3♠	4♠
5♣	?

6. ♠ A 8 3
   ♥ 6 4 2
   ◊ A Q 5 2
   ♣ K J 8

N	S
1♥	3NT
4♣	4♥
4NT	5♥
5NT	?

C. You hold :　　What is your next call in each of these auctions?

	a. You	Ptnr.	**b.** You	Ptnr.	**c.** You	Ptnr
♠ K Q 8 5 3		1♣		1♣		1♣
♡ A Q J 2						
◊ K Q 4	1♠	2♠	1♠	3♠	1♠	4♠
♣ 6	4NT	5♡	4NT	5♠	4NT	5♠
	?		5NT	6◊	5NT	6♡
			?		?	

D. What is your next call in each of these situations?

a. You hold :		You	Ptnr.	**b.** You hold :		You	Ptnr.
♠ K 8 4 3			2♣	♠ K 6 5 2			2♣
♡ Q 9 5 4 2		2♡	2♠	♡ 8 7 5 3		2◊	2♠
◊ A 2		3♠	4♣	◊ 7 2		3♠	4♣
♣ 3 2		?		♣ Q 3 2		?	

c. You hold :		You	Ptnr.	**d.** You hold :		You	Ptnr.
♠ 9 8 4 3			2♣	♠ K J 7 4		1♡	1♠
♡ 9 5 4 2		2◊	2♠	♡ A K Q 9 3		3♠	4♣
◊ A J 7 2		3♠	4♣	◊ 7 2		4♡	5♣
♣ 2		4◊	4♡	♣ Q 3		?	
		?					

PARTNERSHIP BIDDING PRACTICE

When a slam is possible, there may be a number of sensible sequences to reach the slam. West is the dealer on each hand. How might the bidding go?

WEST	EAST	WEST	EAST
65. ♠ A K J 7 4	65. ♠ 10 3	68. ♠ A Q J 7 6	68. ♠ 9 5
♡ A K Q 3	♡ J 8	♡ A Q J 5	♡ K 7 4 3
◊ A J	◊ K Q 6 2	◊ K 3	◊ A Q 7
♣ J 3	♣ K Q 9 7 4	♣ K 9	♣ A J 5 4
66. ♠ Q 8 4	66. ♠ A K 6	69. ♠ J 3 2	69. ♠ 5 4
♡ K J 9 7	♡ A Q 2	♡ Q	♡ A K J 8 2
◊ A K 3	◊ 8 7 4 2	◊ A K J 4 2	◊ 8
♣ 8 7 2	♣ A K Q	♣ A K Q 6	♣ J 9 5 4 2
67. ♠ K 6	67. ♠ A Q J	70. ♠ A J	70. ♠ K 9 4
♡ J 5 3	♡ A K Q 8 7 6	♡ A K Q J 8 4	♡ 5 3 2
◊ 9 7 4 2	◊ A K Q	◊ A K Q 2	◊ 8 7 5
♣ A 8 4 2	♣ K	♣ A	♣ K 8 6 2

TIPS FOR DECLARER

The power of the tenace

How should you play this combination?

> **Dummy :** A J 6 3 2
>
> **You :** K 8 7 5 4

There are only three cards missing and usually they will split 2-1 so that cashing your top cards will capture the ones missing. What about a 3-0 split? Can you cope with that?

When you have winners in both hands, it may make a difference in which order you cash those winners. Where you have a tenace, best technique is to *cash your winners opposite the tenace first.* A tenace is a combination of a high card and a lower card where the opponents hold the card(s) in-between. If it is not clear whether you have a tenace, examine your holding and work out which card is nearest to being a winner. In the above example, the ace and king are winners and the card closest to being a winner is the jack. The A-J combination is the tenace. Therefore, cash the king first. This will gain if the suit lies this way :

```
                    NORTH
                    A J 6 3 2
     WEST                            EAST
     Q 10 9                          - - -
                    SOUTH
                    K 8 7 5 4
```

When you play the king and East shows out, you can now finesse the jack so that West's queen will not make a trick. Had you played the ace first, destroying your tenace, you could no longer have captured the queen. Having a tenace gives you a possible finessing combination. You should note that if the missing cards lie over your tenace, you cannot capture them anyway. If East held Q-10-9, East can make a trick no matter how you play.

```
                    NORTH
                    K 10 4 3
     WEST                            EAST
     J 9 8 5                         7
                    SOUTH
                    A Q 6 2
```

Dummy's K-10 holding is the tenace. Therefore South should start by cashing the ace and queen, the winners opposite the tenace. If the suit divides 3-2, it makes no difference. When it breaks 4-1 and West has J-x-x-x, this precaution pays dividends. When East shows out on the second round, dummy still has the K-10 tenace and South can finesse the 10. Had the king been played on the first or second round, West would make a trick.

(These hands can be made up by using pages 157-160)

Hand 21 : Setting up extra tricks — Catering for a bad break

Dealer North : Nil vulnerable

WEST	NORTH	EAST	SOUTH
	Pass	2NT	Pass
6NT	Pass	Pass	Pass

NORTH
♠ 9 6 5 2
♡ J 10 9 4 3
◇ 6 5 2
♣ 8

WEST
♠ Q J 4
♡ K Q 6
◇ K 7 4
♣ K 9 3 2

EAST
♠ A K 7
♡ A 8 2
◇ A Q 3
♣ Q J 5 4

SOUTH
♠ 10 8 3
♡ 7 5
◇ J 10 9 8
♣ A 10 7 6

Bidding : With 14 points opposite 20 at least, West has enough for slam.

Lead : ◇J, top of sequence.

Play : With 9 tricks outside clubs, 3 club tricks are needed to succeed. As the tenace in clubs is the K-9, start with the honours in the other hand. Win the lead and play the ♣Q. If it wins continue with the ♣J, while if the ♣Q is taken by the ace, win the return and cash the ♣J. When North shows out on the second club, take a finesse of dummy's 9 next time.

Wrong play : Playing winners in the other suits before tackling clubs.

Hand 22 : Leaving the top trump out while you discard a loser

Dealer East : N-S vulnerable

WEST	NORTH	EAST	SOUTH
		Pass	1◇
Pass	1♡	Pass	3♡
Pass	4♣	Pass	4♠
Pass	6♡	All pass	

NORTH
♠ 8 6
♡ K 9 5 3 2
◇ A 2
♣ A K J 5

WEST
♠ J 9 7 5 4 3
♡ 10
◇ 10 9 5 3
♣ 10 4

EAST
♠ K Q 10
♡ Q J 8
◇ 8 4
♣ Q 9 7 6 2

SOUTH
♠ A 2
♡ A 7 6 4
◇ K Q J 7 6
♣ 8 3

Bidding : After 3♡, North has slam prospects but is concerned about the spade situation. 4♣ and 4♠ = cue bids. With the spades under control, North has enough to bid the slam.

Lead : ♠K. In a trump contract, the lead from a K-Q suit is the king.

Play : Win the ♠A. Play the A-K of hearts, the ◇A, a diamond to the king and on the third diamond, pitch your spade loser. East ruffs but the spade loser has been eliminated.

Hand 23 : Rejecting a finesse — Delaying trumps — Discarding a loser

Dealer South : Both vulnerable

NORTH
♠ A K Q J 2
♡ K Q J 4
♢ A Q J
♣ 2

WEST
♠ 10 8
♡ 6
♢ 10 9 8 7 5 4
♣ Q 10 8 7

EAST
♠ 9 6 5 4 3
♡ A 8
♢ K 2
♣ 9 6 5 4

SOUTH
♠ 7
♡ 10 9 7 5 3 2
♢ 6 3
♣ A K J 3

WEST	NORTH	EAST	SOUTH
			Pass
Pass	2♣	Pass	2♡
Pass	4NT	Pass	5♢
Pass	6♡	All pass	

Bidding : South's 2♡ is a positive reply. That is enough for North to check on aces and bid the slam.

Lead : ♢10. Top of sequence.

Play : Win the ♢A, play ♠A-K to discard the diamond loser and then lead trumps. Later the last trump is drawn and losing clubs are ruffed or discarded on the spade winners.

Wrong play : (1) The unnecessary diamond finesse at trick 1.
(2) Playing trumps before taking a discard. East wins ♡A, cashes ♢K.

Hand 24 : Catering for a bad break — Setting up extra winners

Dealer West : Nil vulnerable

NORTH
♠ Q 10 9
♡ J 10 9 8
♢ Q 10 9
♣ 9 6 5

WEST
♠ K 8 6 5 4 2
♡ A
♢ A K 5 4
♣ K 8

EAST
♠ A J 7 3
♡ K Q
♢ 8 7 3
♣ Q J 10 4

SOUTH
♠ - - -
♡ 7 6 5 4 3 2
♢ J 6 2
♣ A 7 3 2

WEST	NORTH	EAST	SOUTH
1♠	Pass	2♣	Pass
2♢	Pass	4♠	Pass
4NT	Pass	5♢	Pass
6♠	Pass	Pass	Pass

Bidding : After East's 4♠, showing support and 13 points or more, West revalues to 21 points, checks on aces and bids the small slam.

Lead : ♡J, top of sequence.

Play : Win the ♡A and play ♠K next. This precaution preserves the A-J tenace in dummy, just in case a finesse becomes necessary. When South shows out, finesse the ♠J, cash the ♠A to draw the last trump and then lead a club to the king and continue with the clubs. Later you can discard two diamond losers.

CHAPTER 9

PRE-EMPTIVE OPENING BIDS

Without interference, most pairs with a little experience can bid well enough to the best spot most of the time. Information is exchanged by the partnership's dialogue. For example, 1♡ : 2♣, 2◇ : 2♡, 4♡ can be translated into: 'I have hearts.' : 'What about clubs?', 'No, I have diamonds, too.' : 'Oh, I prefer your hearts.', 'All right, let's try 4♡ then.'

Imagine that before any of the above dialogue has taken place you started with a 3♠ opening. What will happen to their dialogue? Opening bids of 3-in-a-suit, 3NT, 4-in-a-suit or 5♣ or 5◇ are called pre-empts because by getting in first, you aim to shut out the opponents. Pre-empts force the opposition into guessing what to do. Their decisions have to be made without any clear knowledge of what is held by their partner. When they have to guess at the contract, they will sometimes make the wrong guess. That is your profit.

A pre-emptive bid is made on the first round of bidding. There is no such concept as a pre-emptive rebid, since if the opponents have not been in the bidding on the first round, there is no need to shut them out. A pre-empt can be made in any position, by opener, by responder or by either defender. Pre-empts are more effective the sooner they are made since that reduces the amount of information the opponents can exchange. Therefore, pre-empt as high as you dare as early as possible. Once you have pre-empted, do not bid again unless your partner makes a forcing bid.

A pre-emptive bid skips two or more levels of bidding. For example, an opening bid of 3◇ is a pre-empt because it skips over 1◇ and 2◇. Likewise, 1♣ : 3◇ is a pre-empt because it skips over 1◇ and 2◇. However, 1♠ : 3◇ would not be a pre-empt, as it skips over only one level, the 2◇ bid. The 3◇ response here is a jump-shift, a powerful change of suit.

The normal pre-emptive opening contains :

● **6-10 high card points, and**

● **A strong 7-card or longer suit**

A pre-emptive opening may have fewer than 6 points if it contains the right number of playing tricks (see next page), but in practice, this is very rare. It may also be a very powerful 6-card suit, but this is rare, too. Do not start with a pre-empt if you have a 4-card or longer major as a second suit.

When you have a hand suitable for a pre-empt, you may open with a bid of 3 or a bid of 4 (and if your suit is a minor, you may even begin with a bid of 5♣ or 5◊). How can you judge whether you should open with a 3-bid or with a higher bid? The answer depends on the number of playing tricks you hold. The Rule of 3 and 2 states : *Count your playing tricks and add 3 tricks if not vulnerable, 2 tricks if vulnerable. Make the opening bid which corresponds to this total number of tricks.*

With 6 playing tricks, open 3 if not vulnerable, pass if vulnerable.

With 7 playing tricks, open 4 if not vulnerable, open 3 if vulnerable.

With 8 playing tricks : Not vulnerable, open 4 if your suit is a major and 5 if your suit is a minor. If vulnerable, open 4 in either case.

With 9 playing tricks, open 4 if your suit is a major, 5 if it is a minor.

The 3NT opening shows a 7-card or longer minor headed by A-K-Q and no additional ace, king or queen.

HOW TO COUNT YOUR PLAYING TRICKS

1. Count every card after the third card in a suit as one playing trick.

2. In the top three cards of each suit, each ace and each king = one trick.

3. Count each queen as one trick if there is a second honour card in that suit.

4. Count no trick for a singleton king, singleton queen or queen doubleton. Count only one trick for holding K-Q doubleton.

RESPONDING TO PARTNER'S PRE-EMPTIVE OPENING

1. Assess how many tricks your partner has shown by deducting three if your side is not vulnerable or two if your side is vulnerable.

2. Add to this your own 'quick tricks' : Count the A, K or Q of partner's suit as one trick each. In other suits, count A-K as 2, A-Q as 1½, A as 1, K-Q as 1, and K as ½. If you have support for opener's suit, count an outside singleton as one and an outside void as two.

3. If the total is less than partner's bid or just enough for the contract, pass.

4. If the total is enough for game in partner's suit, you should bid on to game (but if partner's bid is already a game, you would pass). If the total is 12 or more, bid on to a slam provided that you are not missing two aces.

5. Over an opening bid of 3♣ or 3◊, you may try 3NT with a strong balanced hand and at least one stopper in each of the outside suits.

6. Over other opening pre-empts, prefer to stick with partner's suit unless you have a strong hand and a long, powerful suit of your own. A change of suit in response to a pre-empt is forcing.

7. Do not rescue partner from a pre-empt. With a weak hand, pass.

RESPONDING TO PARTNER'S 3NT OPENING

1. Pass with stoppers in both majors and one of the minors.

2. Bid 4♣ with a weak hand and either one major unguarded or both minors unguarded. Partner will bid 4◊ if partner's long suit is diamonds.

3. Bid 5♣ with a strong unbalanced hand. Partner will convert this to 5◊ if partner's long suit is diamonds.

4. With five or more quick tricks including at least two aces, slam is likely. You can count on partner for seven tricks in partner's long minor.

EXERCISES ON PRE-EMPTIVE BIDDING

A. Pre-empts are based on playing trick potential. How many tricks would you expect to win with each of these suits as trumps?

1. A K Q x x x x x	6. A Q J x x x x	11. K x x x x x x x
2. A K Q x x x x	7. A Q x x x x x x	12. K x x x x x x
3. A K Q x x x	8. A x x x x x	13. Q J 10 x x x x
4. A K x x x x x x	9. K Q J x x x x	14. J x x x x x x
5. A K x x x x x	10. K Q x x x x x x	15. x x x x x x x x x

B. You are dealer. What action do you take with these hands if you are :
(i) not vulnerable? (ii) vulnerable?

1. ♠ Q J 10 8 7 4 2 ♡ 5 ◊ K Q J ♣ 5 4	2. ♠ 8 ♡ K Q J 9 7 6 5 4 ◊ 4 3 ♣ 3 2	3. ♠ K 3 ♡ 5 4 ◊ 8 7 ♣ A K J 9 8 6 2
4. ♠ 3 2 ♡ J 6 ◊ A K Q 9 8 7 5 ♣ 5 2	5. ♠ K J 10 7 6 5 4 ♡ 6 ◊ Q J 10 9 6 ♣ - - -	6. ♠ 5 ♡ 4 3 ◊ 7 4 3 2 ♣ A K Q 7 6 4
7. ♠ K Q J 8 7 ♡ 5 ◊ Q J 10 6 ♣ 4 3 2	8. ♠ K 6 3 2 ♡ 9 ◊ 3 ♣ A 8 7 6 4 3 2	9. ♠ J 9 8 6 5 4 ♡ A K 3 ◊ 9 8 7 ♣ 3
10. ♠ 4 ♡ J 9 7 6 4 3 2 ◊ A 2 ♣ J 8 6	11. ♠ A 5 ♡ A K Q 9 7 6 3 ◊ Q 9 7 ♣ 2	12. ♠ 6 5 ♡ A K Q 9 7 6 3 ◊ 9 7 3 ♣ 2

C. Partner opens 3♡. Your response : (i) not vulnerable? (ii) vulnerable?

1. ♠ A J 9 8 7
   ♡ 5 3
   ◇ Q J 7 6
   ♣ 8 5

2. ♠ A J 9 8 6 4
   ♡ 3
   ◇ Q J 7
   ♣ 6 5 2

3. ♠ A K 5 4 3
   ♡ - - -
   ◇ J 8 7 4 3
   ♣ 9 7 6

4. ♠ A K J 8 7 2
   ♡ 5
   ◇ A Q J
   ♣ J 3 2

5. ♠ A 8 7
   ♡ K 8 6 2
   ◇ A 8 4
   ♣ 6 4 3

6. ♠ 7
   ♡ Q 4 3
   ◇ A K 8 4 3
   ♣ J 6 3 2

7. ♠ A Q J
   ♡ 5 4 3
   ◇ Q J 10 6
   ♣ K Q 10

8. ♠ A K 6 5 3 2
   ♡ 4 3
   ◇ A 7
   ♣ Q J 7

9. ♠ A K J 4 3
   ♡ 9 7
   ◇ K Q J 7 6
   ♣ 2

10. ♠ K 8 7 6 4
    ♡ 3
    ◇ A J 7 6 5 2
    ♣ 4

11. ♠ A 5
    ♡ K 7 6 4
    ◇ A 9 7
    ♣ A K Q J

12. ♠ A 6 5
    ♡ K 9 4
    ◇ A K Q 8 7 2
    ♣ 5

PARTNERSHIP BIDDING PRACTICE

West is dealer on each hand, nil vulnerable. How should the bidding go?

WEST	EAST	WEST	EAST
71. ♠ KQJ8643	71. ♠ 10 2	74. ♠ A 7 6	74. ♠ 4
♡ 8 4	♡ A K 6	♡ 7	♡ KQJ8652
◇ 4 3	◇ A K 7 5	◇ A J 8 4 3	◇ 9 6
♣ 9 7	♣ 8 6 5 4	♣ 6 5 4 2	♣ 8 7 3
72. ♠ 8	72. ♠ A Q 3	75. ♠ AQJ96432	75. ♠ K 8 7
♡ 10 6	♡ A J 7 2	♡ 9 4	♡ 7
◇ A Q J 7 6 5 4	◇ 8 3 2	◇ 8	◇ A K 4 3
♣ 7 6 2	♣ A J 10	♣ 9 7	♣ A 8 6 4 3
73. ♠ 9 3	73. ♠ A K 7 6 5 4	76. ♠ 8 2	76. ♠ A K Q
♡ 8	♡ A 9 5	♡ A 4	♡ KQJ7532
◇ A K J 7 5 3 2	◇ 8	◇ K Q 9 7 4 3 2	◇ 6
♣ 9 5 3	♣ A Q 4	♣ 7 5	♣ A Q

TIPS ON DECLARER PLAY

Producing winners with very low cards is the sign of a good player. We have seen that we can make extra tricks by forcing out high cards held by the opponents. It is also possible to produce extra winners by removing all the cards held by the opponents in a suit.

874

J 9 3   10 6 5

A K Q 2

Since the missing cards divide 3-3, after the ace, king and queen have been played, the 2 will be a winner as neither opponent has any cards left.

Sometimes you may need to give up a trick to score extra winners :

7 3

Q J 8   10 6 5

A K 9 4 2

If South plays the ace, king and a third round, the 3-3 division means that there are no opposing cards in the suit. South's last two cards in the suit are now high. As a trick has to be lost anyway, declarer could lose a trick early and cash the ace and king later. This is useful if the South hand has few entries. If some other suit were trumps, South could play the ace, king and then ruff the third round. Again South has two extra winners.

874

Q J 9   K 10

A 6 5 3 2

South has one trick with the ace but can set up two extra tricks by giving up two tricks in the suit. After three rounds have been played, the last two cards in the South hand will be winners.

A K 8 7 3 2

Q J 9   10 6 5

4

If some other suit is trumps, South can play the ace, king and ruff the third round. As the opponents have no more cards in the suit, the last three cards in dummy will be winners. South will need an entry to reach dummy.

A K 8 7 3 2

Q J 9 5   10 6

4

This time, after ace, king and ruff the third round, West still has a card left. Declarer will need to return to dummy in another suit, ruff a fourth round and return again to dummy to use the extra two winners established.

PLAY HANDS ON PRE-EMPTIVE BIDDING

(These hands can be made up by using pages 157-160)

Hand 25 : Shut-out opening — Establishing a second suit in hand

Dealer North : Nil vulnerable

NORTH
♠ A K Q 9 7 6 5
♡ 2
♢ 8
♣ 9 8 7 3

WEST
♠ J 8 3
♡ 10 9 6 5 4
♢ K Q 10
♣ A K

EAST
♠ 10
♡ K Q J 8 3
♢ A J 5
♣ 6 5 4 2

SOUTH
♠ 4 2
♡ A 7
♢ 9 7 6 4 3 2
♣ Q J 10

WEST	NORTH	EAST	SOUTH
	4♠	All pass	

Bidding : With 7 tricks not vulnerable, North has enough to open 4♠ rather than 3♠. Neither East nor West are strong enough to bid over that. Note that if West were the dealer, West would open 1♡ and over North's 4♠ overcall, East would compete to 5♡ which would succeed. North's 4♠ opening has shut East-West out of the game they could make.

Lead : ♡K, top of sequence.

Play : Win ♡A, draw trumps in three rounds and then lead clubs at each opportunity to set up two extra tricks after the ♣A-K are forced out.

Hand 26 : Play from dummy at trick 1 — Establishing a long suit

Dealer East : N-S vulnerable

NORTH
♠ K Q 7 6
♡ K 10 8 7 3
♢ J 9 8
♣ 2

WEST
♠ A 10 9 3
♡ A 6 5
♢ A K 10
♣ 9 5 4

EAST
♠ 4 2
♡ Q 4
♢ 6 3
♣ K Q J 8 7 6 3

SOUTH
♠ J 8 5
♡ J 9 2
♢ Q 7 5 4 2
♣ A 10

WEST	NORTH	EAST	SOUTH
		3♣	Pass
3NT	Pass	Pass	Pass

Bidding : With 6 playing tricks and not vulnerable, East may open 3♣. With a balanced hand, all outside suits covered and four tricks opposite East's six, West should choose 3NT.

Lead : ♡7. Fourth-highest.

Play : Play the ♡Q from dummy, hoping to win the trick (when North has the king). When the ♡Q holds, lead clubs to force out the ace. Once the ♣A has gone, dummy's clubs are high. South should return a heart, partner's suit, but West wins this and cashes the clubs and other winners.

Hand 27 : Slam bidding after a pre-empt — Setting up a long suit

Dealer South : Both vulnerable

NORTH
♠ J
♡ A Q J
♦ K 10 9
♣ A 9 8 7 6 3

WEST
♠ K 6 5 4 3 2
♡ 9 8 6
♦ - - -
♣ K Q J 4

EAST
♠ A Q 10 9 7
♡ K 5 4 3 2
♦ 7
♣ 10 2

SOUTH
♠ 8
♡ 10 7
♦ A Q J 8 6 5 4 3 2
♣ 5

WEST	NORTH	EAST	SOUTH
			4♦
Pass	4NT	Pass	5♦
Pass	6♦	All pass	

Bidding : With 8 tricks vulnerable, South opens 4♦ rather than 3♦. With 3 sure winners and potential for another in three other suits, North bids to slam after checking on aces.

Lead : ♣K. Top of sequence.

Play : The best play is to set up the club suit. Win ♣A, ruff a club high, diamond to dummy's 9, ruff a club, diamond to dummy's 10, ruff a club. The last two clubs in dummy are high. Diamond to the king (or a heart to the ace) and play the clubs on which a spade and a heart are discarded.

Hand 28 : Pre-emptive opening — Counting tricks — Slam bidding

Dealer West : Nil vulnerable

NORTH
♠ 10 6 4 3 2
♡ - - -
♦ K 9 3 2
♣ 10 8 7 6

WEST
♠ 7
♡ A J 10 7 6 3 2
♦ Q J 10
♣ 4 3

EAST
♠ A 9 5
♡ K 8 5 4
♦ A 6
♣ A K Q J

SOUTH
♠ K Q J 8
♡ Q 9
♦ 8 7 5 4
♣ 9 5 2

WEST	NORTH	EAST	SOUTH
3♡	Pass	4NT	Pass
5♦	Pass	7NT	All pass

Bidding : With five playing tricks in hearts and one in diamonds, West opens 3♡ not vulnerable. East has enough for a slam and after finding the missing ace, East counts tricks : 1 in spades, 7 in hearts (given that West has seven hearts to the ace), 1 in diamonds and 4 in clubs. With 13 top winners, choose 7NT, mainly because you eliminate the risk of the opening lead being ruffed.

Lead : ♠K, top of sequence.

Play : Win and play out the hearts, being careful to play the ♡10 early, so that the hearts are not 'blocked'.

CHAPTER 10

OVERCALLS

DOUBLES AND REDOUBLES

In the bidding any player may double a bid made by an opponent. Say 'Double'. If there is no further bidding, the double increases the rewards for success and the penalties for failure. After a double, the other side may redouble (say 'Redouble') increasing the rewards and penalties further.

Any double or redouble is cancelled by a bid, but there may be further doubles and redoubles of later bids. 1♠ making 7 tricks scores 30 but 1♠ doubled and redoubled making 7 tricks scores 120 plus the game bonus plus 100 bonus points for making a redoubled contract. For additional details as to the points scored when the contract is defeated, see page 116.

It seems obvious that you should double only when you are confident of beating the opposition contract, but you will see later that it is normal practice in some circumstances to use a double as a conventional (artificial) request to partner to make a bid.

COMPETITIVE BIDDING STRATEGY

Bidding after the opponents have made a bid is known as 'competitive bidding'. With normal luck, your side will open the bidding only half the time. This chapter and the next are concerned with the actions you may take after the bidding has been opened by the other side.

There is only one opening bid in each auction, the first bid made, and there is only one opening bidder. The partner of the opening bidder is the responder and the opposing side is known as 'the defenders'. A bid made by a defender is an 'overcall' but not an opening. There is no such concept as 'opening for your side' after the other side has made a bid. The principles for competitive bidding are not the same as for opening the bidding and it is essential to appreciate the reasons for the differences.

After an opponent has opened, you may assume that the opener has about 12 HCP or better. It is highly unlikely that your side can now make a slam and your aims are usually much more modest. Your major concerns are whether your side might have enough for a game or a part-score and how to indicate the best defence for partner if the opposition win the bidding.

These are the situations with which you need to deal :

(1) If most of the missing strength is with you and partner, your side may be able to make a game.

(2) If the opponents hold most of the strength, they are likely to bid to a game. Your aim is to indicate a good lead for partner to help the defence.

(3) If the high card strength is roughly equal, each side may be able to make a part-score. Your aim is to compete for the part-score and, if they outbid you, to assist partner in finding the best lead.

While opening the bidding is usually clearcut, the decisions for overcalling are not always straightforward. You may choose to overcall on a hand which you would not open if your suit is very strong and indicates a good lead to partner. This may assist your objectives in (2) and (3) above. On the other hand, you may choose to pass on a hand which you would open if your hand is very strong defensively. Your aim is to score points. If your hand can take as many tricks by defending as by playing, it may pay you to pass on decent hands and simply defend. If they have bid up to 3♣, you need to win only five tricks to defeat them but you need to make nine tricks or more to outbid them.

Note the difference between these hands :

1.	♠ K Q J 10 9 8	2.	♠ A 7 4	3.	♠ K Q 9 7
	♡ 7 6 4		♡ A 6 2		♡ A J 7 5 3
	◇ 6 5		◇ A J 7 5		◇ - - -
	♣ 6 4		♣ 6 4 3		♣ K 9 8 2

Hand 1 is useful only in a spade contract. If spades are trumps, you will win five tricks. If the opponents play in their trump suit, you may take no tricks at all. This hand has excellent *playing strength* but very poor *defence*. If partner is on lead against their contract, a spade lead is perfectly safe. Any other lead from partner might cost a trick.

Hand 2 has three winners. These winners are the same whether you play the hand or whether you are defending. With good defence, there is no urgency to try to play the hand. Balanced hands with no 5-card suit are usually better defensively. Unless you have considerably more strength than the opponents, do not bid on such hands. Pass and defend. Hand 2 is typically a hand that is worth an opening bid but should pass if the opponents open the bidding.

Hand 3 has good playing strength and good defensive strength. It depends on which suit the opposition open. If they start with 1◇, it is very likely that partner will be able to support one of your suits. If so, you have excellent chances of making some contract with a good trump fit. Three-suiters short in the enemy suit have excellent playing potential. However, if they open 1♡ or 1♠, you have excellent defensive values because you are *strong in their suit*. There is also less chance of your side having a trump fit. When strong in the suit opened by the opposition, it often pays to pass and defend.

THE 1NT OVERCALL

This is much stronger than the opening 1NT and shows a balanced hand of 16-18 points with at least one stopper in their suit. The minimum holdings which qualify as a stopper are the ace, K-x, Q-x-x or J-x-x-x, i.e., a holding where if they lead their suit from the top, you will win a trick in that suit. Bidding after the 1NT overcall follows the same structure as after a 1NT opening bid (see Chapter 2), but the points needed to invite game (7-8) or insist on game (9+) are lower as the 1NT overcall is 16-18, not 12-14.

With weaker balanced hands, it is normal to pass even with the values for an opening bid. Firstly, it is sound strategy to pass and defend when your defensive potential is about the same as your playing tricks and your hand is balanced. Secondly, it is much riskier to overcall 1NT after an opening bid by the opposition. As third player knows that opener has about 12 HCP or better, it is easy to make a penalty double of 1NT if third player can tell that their side has more high card strength than your side.

THE SUIT OVERCALL

The great difference between opening the bidding (constructive bidding) and bidding after the opponents have opened (competitive bidding) is this : With 13 points or more, you would always *open* the bidding, yet if they have already opened the bidding, you should pass *unless your hand fits the requirements for an overcall or for a takeout double* (see next chapter). Thus, if they have opened, there is no obligation for you to bid, even if you have 13 points or 15 points or 17 points . . . The most common strong hands on which pass is best are balanced hands up to 15 points (too weak for a 1NT overcall) if they are not suitable for a takeout double, and those hands which have length and strength in a suit bid by the opponents.

While there are no suit quality requirements for *opening* and while you might *open* in a very weak suit, *overcalls in a suit* are based on strongish suits, at least five cards long. The essence of the overcall is the long, strong suit. If your suit is strong, make an overcall even with as few as 8 or 9 high card points. Points are less important than suit quality.

A suit overcall at the 1-level shows :

● **A strong suit, at least five cards long, and**

● **8-15 high card points**

A suit overcall at the 2-level (not a jump-overcall) shows :

● **A strong suit, at least five cards long, and**

● **10-15 high card points**

Thus, an overcall might be as strong as a minimum opening hand, but it need not be that strong, and can be quite weak in high cards. Just how good must a suit be to qualify as a 'strong suit? An excellent guide for overcalls and for pre-emptive openings is the **SUIT QUALITY TEST** :

Count the number of cards in the suit you wish to bid. Add the number of honour cards in that suit (but count the jack or ten as a full honour only if the suit also contains at least one higher honour).

The total is the number of tricks for which you may bid that suit. Thus, if the total is 7, you may bid your suit at the 1-level. If the total is 8, you may bid your suit at the 1-level or the 2-level if necessary. If the total is 9, you may bid your suit at the 1-level, the 2-level or, if necessary, the 3-level.

1.	♠ 7 3 2	2.	♠ 5 2	3.	♠ A 2
	♡ A K 8 7 3		♡ Q 8 6 4 3		♡ 7 5 3
	◊ 9 7		◊ A K		◊ 9 2
	♣ K 8 3		♣ J 7 3 2		♣ A K J 9 8 2

Hand 1 has a decent heart suit with a suit quality of 7 (five cards plus two honours). Over their opening bid of 1♣ or 1◊, it is worth an overcall of 1♡. If their opening bid is 1♠, this suit is not enough for a 2♡ overcall which should indicate a suit quality of 8.

Hand 2 has the same HCP as Hand 1, but the suit quality of the hearts is only 6 (five cards plus one honour). It is not worth even a 1♡ overcall.

The club suit in Hand 3 has a suit quality of 9 (six cards plus 3 honours). It is worth an overcall of 2♣, or if their bidding has already reached the two-level, the hand is good enough for a 3♣ overcall.

RESPONDING TO A SUIT OVERCALL

Below 8 points, you should normally pass unless you have good support for partner. With exactly 8 points, bid if you have something worthwhile to say, otherwise pass.

With 9 or more points, you should find some bid. Raising partner = 8-11 points (but only three trumps are required), a jump-raise would show 12-15 and a raise from the 1-level to game would be based on 16 points or more.

With their suit stopped, you may reply 1NT (9-12 points), 2NT (13-14) or 3NT (15 or more). A change of suit at the 1-level would show 8-15 points and a respectable 5-card suit, while at the 2-level it would show 10-15 points plus a good 5-card or longer suit.

None of the preceding actions is forcing. To force the overcaller to bid again you must jump-shift (jump in a new suit to show 16 or more points and a good 5-card or longer suit) or bid the enemy suit (an artificial forcing bid, called a 'cue bid').

After partner has replied to your overcall you may pass with a minimum overcall if you have nothing worthwhile to add, but keep bidding if —

(a) Partner's reply was forcing, *or*

(b) You have a maximum overcall (in the 13-15 point zone), *or*

(c) You are minimum but you have some extra shape worth showing.

SUMMARY OF RESPONSES TO A SIMPLE OVERCALL

YOUR ACTION	SEQUENCE				EXPECTED HOLDING
Raise partner's suit	N	E	S	W	3+ trump support is adequate
Single raise	1♦	1♠	No	2♠	8-11 points and support
	1♠	2♥	No	3♥	
Double raise	1♦	1♠	No	3♠	12-15 points and support
	1♠	2♥	No	4♥	12+ points and support
Game raise	1♦	1♠	No	4♠	16+ points and support
Bid a new suit					Denies support if partner bid a major
At the one-level	1♦	1♥	No	1♠	8-15 points, denies 3+ hearts
At the two-level	1♦	1♥	No	2♣	10-15 points, denies 3+ hearts
Jump-shift	1♦	1♥	No	2♠	16+ points, 5+ spades, forcing
	1♦	1♥	No	3♣	16+ points, 5+ clubs, forcing
Double jump	1♣	1♦	No	3♥	Pre-emptive, 7+ suit, 6 tricks
Bid no-trumps					Denies support if partner bid a major and promises at least one stopper in their suit
1NT	1♦	1♥	No	1NT	9-12 points
2NT	1♦	1♥	No	2NT	13-14 points
	1♦	2♣	No	2NT	10-13 points (2-level overcall)
3NT	1♦	1♥	No	3NT	15+ points
	1♦	2♣	No	3NT	14+ points (2-level overcall)
Bid the enemy suit	1♦	1♥	No	2♦	Artificial, forcing to game, 16+ points, no good long suit
	1♠	2♥	No	2♠	

THE JUMP-OVERCALL

A jump-overcall is an overcall of one more than the minimum required, for example, (1♣) : 2♡ or (1◊) : 3♣. The jump-overcall shows a good six-card or longer suit and 16 points or more. The hand will usually have 14-17 HCP and thus a total of 16-19 points, counting Length Points. This method is known as strong jump-overcalls.

Other methods which are in use are weak jump-overcalls — 6-10 HCP and a six-card or longer suit — and intermediate jump-overcalls — 12-15 HCP and a six-card or longer suit. You should assume that you are using strong jump-overcalls unless you and your partner have specifically agreed to use one of the other methods.

One-suited hands are normally shown simply by bidding your long suit. However, hands which contain a good five-card suit but which are too strong for a simple overcall are shown by a double first, followed by a bid of your long suit on the next round (see next chapter).

RESPONDING TO A STRONG JUMP-OVERCALL

You should respond to a strong jump-overcall with 6 points or more.

If partner's suit is a major, first priority is to raise that major. Only two trumps are needed to raise a jump-overcall since the suit will be at least six cards long. With 10 points or more, you should raise a major suit jump-overcall from the 2-level to the 4-level. Without support, bid the other major with at least five cards there, or bid no-trumps if you have their suit stopped. Your last choice would be to introduce a minor suit, but if there is nothing else available, bid a long minor.

If partner's suit is a minor, bid a long major as first priority, no-trumps as your second choice and raise the minor or bid the other minor as your last choice. A change of suit in reply to a jump-overcall is forcing. With a strong hand and no clearcut action, you may force partner to keep bidding if you bid the enemy suit, an artificial forcing action.

DOUBLE AND TRIPLE JUMP-OVERCALLS

A double or triple jump-overcall, such as (1♣) : 3♠ or (1◊) : 4♡, is a pre-empt since it skips over two or more levels of bidding. Pre-emptive jump-overcalls follow the same rules as a pre-emptive opening bid. The suit should have at least seven cards and it should be a strong suit, conforming to the **Suit Quality Test**. The Rule of 3 and 2 applies and the usual strength is 6-10 HCP. However, pre-emptive overcalls of 4♡ or 4♠ are more flexible and the strength can be up to 15 HCP (since your bid is already game and slam is so unlikely after they have opened the bidding).

EXERCISES ON OVERCALLS

A. Neither side is vulnerable. Your right-hand opponent opens 1◇. Do you bid or pass on the following hands? If you decide to bid, what bid do you make?

1.	♠ K J 4 2	2.	♠ A 9	3.	♠ 6 3	4.	♠ K Q
	♡ A 7		♡ K Q 8 3		♡ K J 4 3		♡ 9 4 3 2
	◇ Q 5 2		◇ A J 7		◇ 7 4		◇ A K J 9 7
	♣ K J 6 4		♣ Q J 8 2		♣ A Q J 9 3		♣ J 2

B. Nil vulnerable. Right-hand opponent opens 1♣. What action do you take?

1.	♠ K Q 9 7 4 3	2.	♠ K Q J 7 6	3.	♠ K Q 9 7
	♡ 7 6 4		♡ 7		♡ 3
	◇ K 8 2		◇ A 5 4 2		◇ A 8 7 2
	♣ 6		♣ 7 6 5		♣ Q 7 6 3

4.	♠ 7	5.	♠ A	6.	♠ A Q J 10 7 5 4
	♡ A J 7 2		♡ A J 7 2		♡ 6
	◇ A Q J 9 3		◇ J 8 5 3 2		◇ Q 9 5 3
	♣ 7 6 3		♣ Q 9 7		♣ 7

7.	♠ A Q 9 4 2	8.	♠ A Q	9.	♠ A Q
	♡ 7		♡ A K J 7 5 4		♡ 9 7 5 3 2
	◇ A K J 5 3		◇ Q 4 3		◇ K Q
	♣ 6 2		♣ 6 2		♣ Q 8 7 2

C. Both vulnerable. Right-hand opponent opens 1♠. What action do you take?

1.	♠ K 7	2.	♠ K 7	3.	♠ 7 6
	♡ 6 4		♡ A Q		♡ K 4
	◇ A Q J 7 3 2		◇ Q 8 6 3 2		◇ A 5 4
	♣ 7 6 3		♣ Q 9 8 6		♣ A K Q J 7 5

4.	♠ A Q	5.	♠ 7	6.	♠ A K 10 7 4
	♡ 8 5 3		♡ A 10 9 8 6 2		♡ K
	◇ A 5		◇ A K J 2		◇ Q 9 7
	♣ A K Q J 4 3		♣ 8 3		♣ J 8 6 3

7.	♠ - - -	8.	♠ - - -	9.	♠ J 8 6 4
	♡ 7		♡ 7 6 4		♡ 6 2
	◇ K Q J 9 8 6 4 3		◇ K Q J 9 6 5		◇ Q 7
	♣ Q J 10 9		♣ K 9 6 2		♣ A K 8 4 2

D.
N	E	S	W
1◇	No	1♡	?

N-S vul. The bidding has started as on the left. What action should West take on these hands?

1. ♠ A J 7 4
♡ J 5 2
◇ K Q 5 2
♣ A 7

2. ♠ K Q J 8 4
♡ A Q
◇ 5 4 3 2
♣ 7 6

3. ♠ Q J 10 9 7 4 3
♡ 6
◇ - - -
♣ A 8 4 3 2

E.
N	E	S	W
1♠	No	2♣	?

Both vul. The bidding has started as on the left. What action should West take on these hands?

1. ♠ K 6 3 2
♡ Q J 8 2
◇ A K 7
♣ K Q

2. ♠ 6
♡ K Q J 10 9 4 3
◇ K Q 3
♣ A Q

3. ♠ A Q 9 7
♡ A 4 3
◇ 9 2
♣ K Q J 5

F.
N	E	S	W
1♣	1♡	No	?

E-W vul. The bidding has started as on the left. What action should West take on these hands?

1. ♠ K 8 4 3
♡ 7 6
◇ K 7 6 3
♣ 9 4 3

2. ♠ 6
♡ K 8 4 3 2
◇ A K 8 6 5
♣ 7 4

3. ♠ 6 4
♡ K 8 4 3
◇ A 8 5 4 2
♣ 7 2

4. ♠ Q 6
♡ K 8 4
◇ A K 8 5 3
♣ 7 5 2

5. ♠ A 6 5
♡ 3
◇ K Q J 6 4 2
♣ 7 6 3

6. ♠ A 9 7
♡ 7 6
◇ K 10 8 6
♣ Q J 9 4

7. ♠ A J 8
♡ Q 4
◇ J 10 7 4
♣ K Q 10 3

8. ♠ A Q 9 7 4 3
♡ 7 2
◇ K 8 4
♣ 6 3

9. ♠ A Q 8
♡ K 7
◇ Q J 10 7
♣ K Q 8 6

G.
N	E	S	W
1♡	2♠	No	?

Both vul. East's 2♠ is a strong jump-overcall. What action should West take on these hands?

1. ♠ 10 7 6
♡ 9 6
◇ A 8 7 4 2
♣ Q 4 3

2. ♠ K 7 4 2
♡ 4
◇ Q J 9 5
♣ 8 7 5 2

3. ♠ 7 6
♡ K Q 10
◇ 8 7 6 4 2
♣ Q 10 3

4. ♠ 7 6
♡ K Q 10
◇ A 8 7 4
♣ Q 7 4 3

5. ♠ 10
♡ Q 9
◇ A Q J 7 4 2
♣ 7 6 4 2

6. ♠ 5 3
♡ J 6 3
◇ A K 4 2
♣ Q J 3 2

PARTNERSHIP BIDDING PRACTICE
FEATURING OVERCALLS

Neither side is vulnerable. There is no North-South bidding other than shown.

WEST	EAST	WEST	EAST
77.	**77.**	**82.**	**82.**
S. opens 1♣.	S. opens 1♣.	N. opens 1♥.	N. opens 1♥.
♠ A J 8	♠ K Q 3	♠ A J	♠ K Q 9 7 6 2
♡ K Q 9 8 6 3	♡ 7 5	♡ 7 5 4 2	♡ 9 3
◊ 7 6 2	◊ J 9 8 3	◊ K Q 3	◊ A 8
♣ 8	♣ A 9 7 4	♣ 8 6 4 2	♣ A K 5
78.	**78.**	**83.**	**83.**
S. opens 1♣.	S. opens 1♣.	N. opens 1♥.	N. opens 1♥.
♠ A Q 7	♠ K J	♠ Q J 7 6 4	♠ A 9 3
♡ K Q	♡ J 10 9 7 4 2	♡ 7	♡ 6 2
◊ A 9 8 3	◊ K Q 6 2	◊ Q 9 3	◊ A K J 8 7 4
♣ Q 8 7 2	♣ 3	♣ A J 8 6	♣ 9 3
79.	**79.**	**84.**	**84.**
N. opens 1◊.	N. opens 1◊.	S. opens 1♠.	S. opens 1♠.
♠ A 7 6	♠ K 8 3	♠ 7 5	♠ K 8 4 2
♡ K Q 3	♡ A J 10 7 6 4	♡ A 8 3	♡ K 9 7
◊ J 8 7 4	◊ A Q	◊ 7 6	◊ A J 5 2
♣ 7 3 2	♣ Q 4	♣ A K J 9 3 2	♣ Q 8
80.	**80.**	**85.**	**85.**
N. opens 1◊.	N. opens 1◊.	N. opens 1♠.	N. opens 1♠.
♠ K Q J	♠ A 7 4	♠ 6 4 3 2	♠ 9
♡ 9 8 5 2	♡ K Q J 7 3	♡ A 8	♡ K Q J 7 5 4
◊ Q 3	◊ K 8 4	◊ K Q 7	◊ A 6 3
♣ A J 8 5	♣ 7 3	♣ 9 8 4 2	♣ K Q J
81.	**81.**	**86.**	**86.**
S. opens 1♡.	S. opens 1♡.	N. opens 1♠.	N. opens 1♠.
♠ K Q 8	♠ 7 6 5	♠ A Q	♠ 7
♡ A Q	♡ 8 4 3	♡ A J 6	♡ K 9 2
◊ 7 6 4 2	◊ A Q	◊ K Q 9 4	◊ J 8 2
♣ A K 9 3	♣ Q 7 5 4 2	♣ 9 5 3 2	♣ K Q J 8 7 4

TIPS ON DEFENCE

Leading partner's suit

It is usually a sound move to lead a suit bid by partner. This is particularly so when partner has made an overcall since then the suit figures to be strong. When leading partner's suit, the correct card is the same as though you were leading an unbid suit. Check with the Opening Leads Table on page 139.

Quite often you will be short in partner's suit and with just two or three cards, the card to lead is chosen according to these rules.

1. From a doubleton : Lead the top card.

If partner plays high-low (a lower card on the second round than the card led), this usually indicates that partner has led a doubleton.

2. From three cards, the lead depends on whether you hold an honour.

(a) With no honour card, lead the middle card. From 8 5 2, lead the 5. On the next round, follow with the higher card, the 8. Partner should notice that you have played low-then-high and therefore can deduce that you have not led a doubleton. With a doubleton, the order is high-then-low.

(b) With an honour card and the one immediately below it, lead the top of the touching cards. From Q J 3, lead the queen, from K J 10, the jack.

(c) With an honour card but no touching card below it, lead bottom. From K 7 2, lead the 2, from J 8 5, the 5. If partner can tell that the lead is your lowest possible card, partner will know you do not have a doubleton (lead top from a doubleton) and you do not have just rag cards (from three rags, lead the middle card, not the lowest). Lowest card indicates that either partner has led a singleton or partner holds an honour card in the suit led.

3. With 4+ cards in partner's suit, lead top of sequence or fourth-highest without a sequence : see Appendix 3, on page 139, for specific details.

Third Hand High

After partner has led and dummy has played, if partner's card will not win the trick and you can win the trick, it is usually correct to play your winning card. For example :

8 7 3 2

Q J 10 5   A 9 4

K 6

West leads the queen, top of sequence. East knows that the king must be with South (as the queen lead denies the king). Since West's queen will not win the trick, East should play the ace.

Returning partner's lead

It is often a sensible move to return the suit led by partner but if you have a better plan or you can see that returning partner's suit is futile, be prepared to switch to a suit which might bring in more tricks.

PLAY HANDS ON OVERCALLS AND DEFENCE
(These hands can be made up by using pages 157-160)

Hand 29 : Overcall — Leading partner's suit — Creating a void

Dealer North : Nil vulnerable

NORTH
- ♠ A K
- ♡ K 8 6 2
- ◇ K Q 10 9 3
- ♣ 10 5

WEST
- ♠ 10 9 8
- ♡ 4 3
- ◇ 8 7 6 5 2
- ♣ K 7 2

EAST
- ♠ 6 5 4 3
- ♡ 9 5
- ◇ A
- ♣ A Q J 8 6 3

SOUTH
- ♠ Q J 7 2
- ♡ A Q J 10 7
- ◇ J 4
- ♣ 9 4

WEST	NORTH	EAST	SOUTH
	1◇	2♣	2♡
Pass	4♡	All pass	

Bidding : East's suit is excellent and warrants the overcall. South's 2♡ shows 10 points or better so that North, worth 17 points in support of hearts, has no trouble raising to 4♡.

Lead : ♣2. Lead bottom from three or four to an honour.

Play : East should win ♣A, cash the ◇A to create a void and lead a low club. West wins the ♣K and East ruffs the diamond return. This plan would also work if West's ♣2 lead were a singleton, but if West wrongly led the king of clubs, 4♡ makes.

Hand 30 : Raising an overcall — Reading the lead — Creating a void

Dealer East : Nil vulnerable

NORTH
- ♠ 6 5
- ♡ 2
- ◇ J 7 6 4 3
- ♣ J 7 5 4 2

WEST
- ♠ K J 10 9 3
- ♡ K 9
- ◇ 10 5 2
- ♣ A Q 8

EAST
- ♠ Q 8 4 2
- ♡ Q J 10 7
- ◇ Q 9 8
- ♣ K 9

SOUTH
- ♠ A 7
- ♡ A 8 6 5 4 3
- ◇ A K
- ♣ 10 6 3

WEST	NORTH	EAST	SOUTH
		Pass	1♡
1♠	Pass	2♠	All pass

Bidding : As the top limit for an overcall is 15 HCP, East raises only to 2♠. Nobody should push higher.

Lead : ♡2. Partner's suit is normal.

Play : Winning ♡A, South notes that partner's lead must be a singleton, as there is only one other heart missing. With a doubleton, partner would have led the top card, not the bottom. South cashes the top diamonds (king-then-ace to show a doubleton), creating a void, and leads a heart for North to ruff. South ruffs the diamond return and the ♠A means one off.

Hand 31 : Raising an overcall — Third hand high — Finding a switch

Dealer South : Nil vulnerable

WEST	NORTH	EAST	SOUTH
			1♡
Pass	2♡	2♠	3♡
3♠	Pass	Pass	Pass

NORTH
♠ 5 2
♡ A 9 3 2
◊ 8 2
♣ J 9 8 6 4

WEST
♠ Q 10 3
♡ 8 5 4
◊ J 10 9 4
♣ K Q 7

EAST
♠ A K J 9 8 4
♡ K
◊ K 7 5
♣ 10 5 3

SOUTH
♠ 7 6
♡ Q J 10 7 6
◊ A Q 6 3
♣ A 2

Bidding : East has enough for 2♠ and South should compete to 3♡. Do not sell out at the two-level with a trump fit. 3♡ would succeed but West raises partner to 3♠. 3 trumps are enough to raise an overcall.

Lead : ♡Q. Top of sequence.

Play : Deducing that East holds the ♡K, North plays the ace. When the ♡K drops, it is clear that continuing hearts is futile. North switches to the ◊8 (lead top card from a doubleton). South wins and continues diamonds, North ruffing on the third round, and the ace of clubs defeats the contract.

Hand 32 : Reading the lead — Third hand high — Finding the switch

Dealer West : Nil vulnerable

WEST	NORTH	EAST	SOUTH
Pass	1♡	2◊	2♡
Pass	4♡	All pass	

NORTH
♠ A K
♡ A 10 9 8 5 2
◊ K 3
♣ K J 10

WEST
♠ 8 7 5 4 3 2
♡ 7 4
◊ A 7 5
♣ 9 4

EAST
♠ Q 6
♡ J
◊ Q J 10 9 6 4
♣ A Q 8 7

SOUTH
♠ J 10 9
♡ K Q 6 3
◊ 8 2
♣ 6 5 3 2

Bidding : East's good suit justifies the 2◊ overcall. West is too weak to raise to 3◊. After receiving support, North revalues to 20 points.

Lead : ◊Q, top of sequence.

Play : From the lead, West can tell that declarer holds the ◊K and so West plays the ◊A (third hand high). When the ◊K does not fall, West sees there are no more tricks from that suit for the defence. If returning partner's suit is clearly futile, it is usually better to switch. West shifts to clubs, 9-then-4 (doubleton), and ruffs the third club to defeat 4♡.

CHAPTER 11

TAKEOUT DOUBLES

Two basic types of doubles are commonly used : the Penalty Double *which asks partner to pass* (and aims to collect larger penalties by defeating the opponents' contract) and the Takeout Double *which asks partner to bid* (and aims to find a decent contract for your side). As the meanings are opposite, you must know when partner's double is for takeout and when it is for penalties.

In standard methods, a double is for penalties if :

● **It is a double of a no-trump bid,** *or*

● **If partner has already made a bid,** *or*

● **It is a double at the three-level or higher.**

The general rule is that a double is for takeout if it is a double of a suit bid at the one-level or the two-level and partner has not bid. A takeout double is usually made at the first opportunity, but this need not be so. You may open the bidding or overcall initially and still make a takeout double at your next turn, provided that the above conditions for a takeout double are met.

It is sensible to consider the takeout double as an overcall showing the unbid suits. Thus, if they have bid one suit and you double for takeout, you are showing a three-suiter, the three unbid suits. If they have bid two suits and you double, e.g., (1◊) : No : (1♡) : Double, you are showing the other two suits, spades and clubs in the example auction. What if they have bid one suit and you have only a two-suiter? Now it is better to forego the double. Bid the longer of your two suits (choose the higher suit with a 5-5 pattern) and hope for an opportunity to show your other suit later. With a one-suiter, make an overcall or a strong jump-overcall. If the hand is strong but does not fit a strong jump-overcall, double and bid your suit next round.

WHAT YOU NEED TO MAKE A TAKEOUT DOUBLE

A takeout double has point count requirements *and* shape requirements. The more strength you have, the more you may depart from the requirements of shape, but for a minimum strength double, the shape factors are vital.

When valuing your hand for a takeout double, count high card points and add 3-2-1 points for a shortage in the opposition's suit : 3 for a void, 2 for a singleton and 1 for a doubleton. If your hand now measures 13 points or better, you have the minimum strength needed for a double.

The shape requirements for a takeout double are a shortage in the enemy suit (doubleton or shorter) plus support (four cards) in each unbid suit. It is permissible to have tolerance (three cards) in one of the unbid suits. Thus, if partner doubles one major, expect partner to have four cards in the other major, while if partner doubles a minor suit, expect at least 4-3 in the major suits. Holding both majors, double with 4-4 or 5-4 in the majors, but prefer to overcall with 5-3 in the majors when the 5-card suit is strong.

Where the opponents have bid two suits, a takeout double shows support for both unbid suits. Where the doubler is a passed hand, the takeout double shows 9-11 HCP plus support for any unbid suit. If the doubler has 16 HCP or more, the shape requirements are eased : the doubler need not have a shortage in the enemy suit and need have only tolerance in the unbid suits rather than support. Where the doubler has 19 HCP or more, there are no shape requirements for the double.

RESPONDING TO PARTNER'S TAKEOUT DOUBLE

You are expected to answer partner's takeout double no matter how weak a hand you have. The only time you might elect to pass a takeout double, and thus convert it to a penalty double, is when you have better trumps in your hand than the opponent who bid that suit. (Normally, you would need at least five trumps including three honours to pass out a takeout double.) For practical purposes, take partner's takeout double as forcing.

If you intend to bid a suit in answer to the double, count your HCP and add 5-3-1 Ruffing Points (5 for a void, 3 for a singleton, 1 for a doubleton). If you intend to bid no-trumps, count only your high card points. After you have assessed the value of your hand, these are your options :

0-5 points   : Bid a suit at the cheapest possible level.

6-9 points   : Bid a suit at the cheapest possible level or bid 1NT.

10-12 points : Make a jump bid in a suit or bid 2NT.

13 points or more : Bid a game or bid the enemy suit to force to game.

When responding to a takeout double, ask yourself first 'What shall I bid?' and after you have the answer to that, ask 'How high shall I bid it?'

A suit response at the cheapest level has a range of 0-9 points (including points for distribution). With the upper end of this range (6-9), try to bid a second time if a convenient opportunity arises. You should not let the opponents buy the contract at the one-level or two-level if partner has doubled and your side has a certain or likely trump fit.

If third player bids over partner's takeout double, and thus removes it, the obligation to reply to the double ceases. In such a case you should pass with 0-5 points and make your normal reply with 6 points or more.

The order of priority when responding to a takeout double is :

- **Bid a major first.** Prefer a major suit to a longer or better minor.

- **With no major available, choose a no-trumps response if possible.**

For a no-trumps response, you need at least one stopper in the enemy suit and some high card strength (6-9 points for 1NT). When you hold just 0-5 points, choose a suit bid. The 1NT response is not garbage. With two stoppers, choose the no-trump response but with just one stopper, you may choose a minor suit response if the minor suit is respectable.

- **If unable to bid a major or no-trumps, bid a minor.**

REBIDS BY THE DOUBLER

(a) After a reply showing 0-9 points : The doubler revalues the hand if a trump fit is located, adding the 5-3-1 ruffing point count to the high card points. Then with 13-16 points, the doubler should pass. With 17-19 points, the doubler should bid again, and with 20-22 points, the doubler should make a jump rebid. When the doubler bids again, partner should keep bidding with the 6-9 point hand and pass with 0-5, while if the doubler has made a jump rebid, partner should bid to game if holding one sure trick.

(b) After a jump-response showing 10-12 points : Pass with just 12-13 points, but bid on with 14 points or more and head for a game with 16 or more.

(c) A second bid by the doubler is always strong. A new suit by the doubler shows a 5-card or longer suit and denies support for partner's suit. It is strong but may lack the 6-card suit needed for the strong jump-overcall.

A minimum no-trumps rebid by the doubler shows 19-21 points and a balanced hand (since with 16-18 balanced, you would make an immediate overcall of 1NT, while with 13-15 you should not bid again after doubling if partner has shown 0-9 points).

A new suit by the doubler is not forcing if partner has shown 0-9 points, but is forcing if partner made a reply showing 10-12 points.

ACTION BY THIRD HAND AFTER A TAKEOUT DOUBLE

After partner has opened and second player makes a takeout double, third player should pass on a weak hand, bid in the normal way with 6 points or better and redouble with 10 HCP or more and no fit for opener's suit.

After the redouble, the partner of the doubler should make the normal reply (as the redouble has not removed the double) and the opener should usually pass, unless the hand is suitable to double the last bid for penalties. As the redouble promises another bid, the opener can pass in safety, even with a good hand, knowing that the redoubler will bid again. After a redouble any double by the opener or the redoubler is a penalty double. The function of the redouble is to confirm that your side has more points than they do and thus you can capitalise on the jeopardy in which the opponents find themselves.

EXERCISES ON TAKEOUT DOUBLES

A. In the following auctions, is West's double for takeout or for penalties?

1. N	E	S	W	2. N	E	S	W	3. N	E	S	W
No	No	1♡	Dble	1◇	No	1♠	Dble	1♡	No	2♡	Dble

4. N	E	S	W	5. N	E	S	W	6. N	E	S	W
	1♡	4♠	Dble		No	1NT	Dble		1NT	2♠	Dble

B. Nil vul. North opens 1♣. What action should East take on these hands?

1. ♠ K 8 4 3	2. ♠ A J 8 7	3. ♠ A Q 8 7
♡ Q J 4 2	♡ Q 9 4 3	♡ 6
◇ A Q 7 2	◇ A 10 7 4 3	◇ A K 10 4 3 2
♣ 5	♣ - - -	♣ 6 2

4. ♠ A K J 4	5. ♠ A Q J 9 6 5	6. ♠ A Q 8 7 5
♡ A J 9 6 3	♡ K Q J	♡ 6
◇ K 2	◇ A K	◇ A K 10 4 3
♣ 7 4	♣ 5 2	♣ 4 3

7. ♠ A J 9 7	8. ♠ A J 6 2	9. ♠ A 7
♡ K Q 9	♡ K Q 7	♡ K J 2
◇ A 8 4 3	◇ J 9 6	◇ A Q J 5
♣ 6 3	♣ A Q 5	♣ K Q 3 2

C. Both vul. North opens 1♡. What action should East take on these hands?

1. ♠ K J	2. ♠ K Q	3. ♠ K Q 7 2
♡ A 8	♡ A 4 3	♡ A 3
◇ Q 4 3 2	◇ A 8 3 2	◇ A 8 3 2
♣ Q 9 6 3 2	♣ J 7 5 4	♣ J 7 5

4. ♠ A K 10 9 6	5. ♠ J 8 3 2	6. ♠ K
♡ 3	♡ 6	♡ A K 10 9 6 2
◇ A 5 4	◇ A K 7 6 2	◇ A 7 4
♣ Q 8 6 3	♣ K Q 9	♣ J 4 3

7. ♠ A Q	8. ♠ A Q	9. ♠ A Q J 6 2
♡ K 9 3	♡ K 9 3	♡ A 4
◇ A J 4 3	◇ A K 4 3	◇ A K J 5
♣ K 8 7 4	♣ K J 7 4	♣ Q 3

D.

N	E	S	W
1◇	Dble	No	?

Nil vul. The bidding has started as on the left. What action should West take on these hands?

1. ♠ K 9 7 3
   ♥ Q 5
   ◇ 7 6 4 3
   ♣ 8 3 2

2. ♠ 9 7 3 2
   ♥ 8 4 2
   ◇ 7 6
   ♣ 9 6 4 2

3. ♠ Q 9 8 7 4
   ♥ Q 8 6 5
   ◇ 4 3
   ♣ 6 2

4. ♠ 6 2
   ♥ Q 8 6 5
   ◇ 4 3
   ♣ Q 9 8 7 4

5. ♠ A 7 6
   ♥ 9 2
   ◇ 4 3 2
   ♣ J 9 8 6 3

6. ♠ 7 6 4
   ♥ 5 4 3
   ◇ 7 6 4 3 2
   ♣ 3 2

E.

N	E	S	W
1♣	Dble	No	?

E-W vul. The bidding has started as on the left. What action should West take on these hands?

1. ♠ K 9 8 4 3
   ♥ 6
   ◇ 6 4 2
   ♣ A 7 4 2

2. ♠ K 9 5 4
   ♥ A J 10 7 5
   ◇ 4 3
   ♣ 6 2

3. ♠ 7 6
   ♥ K 8 4
   ◇ A Q J 4 2
   ♣ 6 5 3

4. ♠ J 8 4
   ♥ A 7 3
   ◇ 8 5 3 2
   ♣ Q J 5

5. ♠ 8 5
   ♥ A 7 2
   ◇ A J 9 3
   ♣ Q 10 8 7

6. ♠ K Q 8 7 4 3
   ♥ A 8
   ◇ 2
   ♣ 7 6 4 3

F.

N	E	S	W
1◇	Dble	1♠	?

E-W vul. The bidding has started as on the left. What action should West take on these hands?

1. ♠ Q 7
   ♥ Q 8 4 3
   ◇ 9 6 2
   ♣ 8 6 5 2

2. ♠ 7 2
   ♥ Q J 8 4
   ◇ 8 6 5
   ♣ K J 8 7

3. ♠ 9
   ♥ A J 9 8 5
   ◇ 7 6 2
   ♣ K 8 7 2

G.

N	E	S	W
No	No	1◇	Dble
No	1♥	No	?

N-S vul. The bidding has started as on the left. What action should West take on these hands?

1. ♠ A J 7 4
   ♥ K Q 4 2
   ◇ 7 6
   ♣ K 8 2

2. ♠ A J 7 4
   ♥ K Q 4 2
   ◇ 7 6
   ♣ A K 3

3. ♠ A 8 2
   ♥ A K Q 3
   ◇ 6
   ♣ K Q 9 8 2

PARTNERSHIP BIDDING PRACTICE
FEATURING TAKEOUT DOUBLES

Neither side is vulnerable. There is no North-South bidding other than shown.

WEST	EAST	WEST	EAST
87.	**87.**	**92.**	**92.**
N. opens 1♥.	N. opens 1♥.	N. opens 1♥.	N. opens 1♥.
♠ J 7	♠ K Q 4 3	♠ K J 7	♠ A Q 9 3
♥ 8 6 5 4 2	♥ 7	♥ A J 10	♥ 7 2
◇ Q 7 5 3	◇ A J 8 6	◇ 7 6 3	◇ A 9 2
♣ J 10	♣ Q 9 8 3	♣ 8 7 4 2	♣ A Q J 5
88.	**88.**	**93.**	**93.**
S. opens 1♥.	S. opens 1♥.	S. opens 1♠.	S. opens 1♠.
♠ A K 7 6	♠ 10 8 4	♠ 7	♠ A 8 5 2
♥ 8 3	♥ 9 7 6	♥ A Q 8 3	♥ J 10 2
◇ A Q 9	◇ 4 3	◇ K Q 9 3	◇ A 7 4
♣ J 7 6 4	♣ K 9 5 3 2	♣ A J 9 2	♣ Q 8 3
89.	**89.**	**94.**	**94.**
S. opens 1♣.	S. opens 1♣.	S. opens 1♥.	S. opens 1♥.
♠ A K J 6	♠ Q 9 4 3	♠ A 8 6 2	♠ K Q 9 7 5
♥ K Q J 4	♥ 8 7	♥ 7 4	♥ A 2
◇ A 4 3	◇ 9 8 5 2	◇ A K 6 2	◇ 7 4 3
♣ 9 2	♣ 8 7 6	♣ J 8 5	♣ 9 6 3
90.	**90.**	**95.**	**95.**
N. opens 1♣.	N. opens 1♣.	N. opens 1♣.	N. opens 1♣.
♠ 9 7	♠ A K 5 2	♠ K Q J 6 5 2	♠ A 7 4 3
♥ 6 5 4 2	♥ K Q J 7 3	♥ 7 5	♥ A 9 8 2
◇ 7 6 4	◇ K Q	◇ K J	◇ A 5 4 3
♣ J 8 3 2	♣ 9 7	♣ Q 6 2	♣ 7
91.	**91.**	**96.**	**96.**
N. opens 1◇.	N. opens 1◇.	S. opens 1◇.	S. opens 1◇.
♠ K Q 8 7	♠ A 9 6 3	♠ A K J 7	♠ 6 4
♥ 7 6	♥ K Q 8 5	♥ A 10 9 6 2	♥ K 8 3
◇ 5 4	◇ 9 6	◇ 9	◇ J 6 5
♣ 8 6 4 3 2	♣ A 7 5	♣ A 6 2	♣ K Q J 8 3

TIPS ON DECLARER PLAY

Leading towards honours

Unless you have a solid sequence of high cards, it is usually best to lead towards the honour cards with which you hope to win tricks.

    (a)   **K Q J 10**   (b) **K Q J 4**

           6 5 3 2   **6 5 3 2**

With (a) it does not matter from which hand you lead first, but with (b) it may be vital to lead low from the South hand towards dummy's honours.

K Q J 4

A   **10 9 8 7**

6 5 3 2

In this layout, if the first lead comes from South, the ace goes in and dummy's honours can capture the remaining cards. If the first lead is from the North hand, leading an honour to knock out the ace, there is a second loser later to East.

Card-Reading

♡ **K J 7 2**

♡ **A 10 4 3**

How should you play this combination? With eight cards missing the queen the best play is to take a finesse on the second round. You could cash the ace and then finesse the jack or cash the king and finesse the ten, but which way? If you know which player holds the queen, the problem is solved.

Sometimes it is possible to work out where the missing cards are by counting points. Count the HCP in dummy and add the HCP in your hand. Deduct this from 40 and you have the HCP held by the opponents. You may be able to work out which opponent has all or most of the missing HCP.

Here are some guidelines :

1. Assume that a player who opens the bidding holds 12 HCP or more.

2. Assume a player who fails to open the bidding holds below 12 HCP.

3. Assume a player who was too weak to respond has below 6 HCP.

4. If one opponent has pre-empted, the critical high cards missing in the other suits will usually be with the partner of the pre-empter.

In the example above, if West has pre-empted in clubs, say, assume that the queen of hearts is with East. If East is the pre-empter, play for the queen of hearts to be with West.

PLAY HANDS ON TAKEOUT DOUBLES

(These hands can be made up by using pages 157-160)

Hand 33 : Leading towards honour cards with three honours missing

Dealer North : Nil vulnerable

NORTH
♠ J 10 8 7 4 3
♡ 6
♢ 10 9 5
♣ J 5 3

WEST
♠ K Q 6 5
♡ K Q 5 4
♢ A J 6 4
♣ 4

EAST
♠ A 2
♡ 9 8 7 3 2
♢ K 3
♣ Q 10 6 2

SOUTH
♠ 9
♡ A J 10
♢ Q 8 7 2
♣ A K 9 8 7

WEST	NORTH	EAST	SOUTH
	Pass	Pass	1♣
Dble	Pass	2♡	Pass
4♡	Pass	Pass	Pass

Bidding : East's 2♡ jump reply to the double shows 10-12 points.

Lead : ♣A, normal from A-K suits.

Play : South switches to the ♠9. East wins in hand and leads a heart to the K, winning. As South is marked with the ♡A, do not lead a second heart from dummy. A diamond goes to the king and another heart is led *towards* dummy. This holds the defence to just one trump trick. One club loser can be ruffed later and another discarded on the third spade.

Hand 34 : Delaying trumps to take a quick discard

Dealer East : E-W vulnerable

NORTH
♠ 8
♡ K J 10 6 5 4
♢ A 6
♣ J 9 6 2

WEST
♠ Q 9 7 2
♡ 7
♢ 10 9 7 3
♣ 10 8 5 3

EAST
♠ J 5 4 3
♡ A Q 2
♢ K Q J 8 4
♣ Q

SOUTH
♠ A K 10 6
♡ 9 8 3
♢ 5 2
♣ A K 7 4

WEST	NORTH	EAST	SOUTH
		1♢	Dble
Pass	4♡	All pass	

Bidding : North is worth 13 points (counting 3 for the singleton and 1 for the doubleton). With 13 points or more opposite a takeout double, you should reach game and 4♡ is the clear choice.

Lead : ♢K. Prefer the sequence.

Play : Win ♢A, play the ♠A and ♠K to discard the diamond loser and then lead a trump, finessing the jack . or 10. Declarer should keep on with trumps until all trumps are drawn. West should hold on to the clubs ('keep length with dummy'). When East shows out on the second club, North finesses the ♣9 if necessary.

Hand 35 : Signalling with a doubleton — Card-reading by declarer

Dealer South : Both vulnerable

NORTH
♠ A K Q J
♡ A 7 5 3
♢ K
♣ Q 10 9 8

WEST
♠ 8 5
♡ Q 9
♢ Q J 7 5 2
♣ A K 5 3

EAST
♠ 10 9 7 4 2
♡ 10 8 6
♢ 10 9 3
♣ J 4

SOUTH
♠ 6 3
♡ K J 4 2
♢ A 8 6 4
♣ 7 6 2

WEST	NORTH	EAST	SOUTH
			Pass
1◇	Dble	Pass	1♡
Pass	3♡	Pass	4♡
Pass	Pass	Pass	

Bidding : North's 3♡ is a strong invitation and South has more than enough to bid the game.

Lead : ♣A. A-K leads are attractive.

Play : East signals with the ♣J to continue clubs and ruffs the third club. Hoping West has the ◇A, East exits in diamonds, won in dummy. With only 13 HCP out, South places West, the opener, with the rest of the high cards. Refusing the normal finesse for the queen when holding eight trumps, South plays the ♡A, ♡K. Luckily, the ♡Q drops.

Hand 36 : Card-reading — Finessing — Careful use of entries

Dealer West : Both vulnerable

NORTH
♠ K Q J 10 7
♡ K 8 6 2
♢ 9 4
♣ A 10

WEST
♠ A 9 3 2
♡ 7 4 3
♢ K J 8
♣ Q J 5

EAST
♠ 5
♡ A Q J 10
♢ A Q 5 2
♣ K 8 7 2

SOUTH
♠ 8 6 4
♡ 9 5
♢ 10 7 6 3
♣ 9 6 4 3

WEST	NORTH	EAST	SOUTH
Pass	1♠	Dble	Pass
2NT	Pass	3NT	All pass

Bidding : West's 2NT denies four hearts and shows 10-12 points, balanced, with at least one stopper in spades. East has enough to try for game and 3NT looks the best bet.

Lead : ♠K, to set up the spades.

Play : After winning the ♠A, West should realise it is futile to go for the clubs. North will win and cash the rest of the spades. As only 13 HCP are missing, North is marked with the ♡K for the opening bid. So, finesse the ♡Q, diamond to the jack, finesse ♡J, diamond to the king, finesse ♡10 and you have 9 tricks.

CHAPTER 12

PENALTY DOUBLES

When you are confident that you can defeat the opponents' contract, it is highly attractive to double them. The bonus points for penalties mount up quickly if you beat them by more than one trick. If they are not vulnerable, you collect 50 points for every trick by which they fail, but if you have doubled them, you collect 100 for one down, 300 for two down, 500 for three down and 300 for each additional trick. If they are vulnerable, it is even more lucrative. Undoubled they lose only 100 per trick. Doubled, they lose 200 for one down and 300 for each additional trick. Three down doubled not vulnerable or two down doubled vulnerable = 500, as much as the bonus for a small slam not vulnerable.

On the other hand, if they make their contract doubled, they score double points, plus 50 for the insult of being doubled. Overtricks made when doubled are more valuable than usual : 100 points per overtrick when not vulnerable and 200 points per overtrick when vulnerable. Consider also that if they redouble and make it, the preceding scores are doubled again. Therefore, be confident you can defeat them before you double.

When To Double Their 1NT Opening

You should hold at least as many points as they do. If they are using the weak 1NT (12-14 HCP or 13-15 HCP) double if you hold 15 HCP or more. If they are using the strong 1NT (15-17 HCP or 16-18 HCP), double if holding 17 HCP or more. Partner is expected to pass your double, but with a dreadful hand and a long suit, partner is permitted to remove your double and bid the long suit. This removal of the penalty double is done only on a very weak hand. If either opponent bids a suit after their 1NT has been doubled, you or partner should double this with a strong 4-card or better holding in that suit.

When To Double Their 1NT Overcall

When partner has opened and second player overcalls 1NT, double if your side has more points than they do. If they are trying for more than half the tricks with less than half the points, they will usually fail. Therefore, to maximise your score, double their 1NT overcall whenever you hold 9 HCP or better. Again, after their 1NT has been doubled, if either opponent tries to escape by bidding a suit, you or partner should double this rescue attempt with a strong 4-card holding in that suit.

When To Double Their Suit Overcall At The One-Level

To extract a decent penalty at the one-level, you need excellent trumps. To defeat them at all, you have to take seven tricks. This is equivalent to making a contract of one or more in their suit with a known bad break. Consequently, your trumps should be better than theirs and the minimum recommended is five trumps with three honours. It is helpful to have a shortage in the suit partner opened (so that partner's winners in that suit are unlikely to be ruffed) and at least 20 HCP for your side.

When To Double Their Suit Overcall At The Two-Level

The requirements are slightly less but you should still be strong in their trump suit. For a double at the 2-level you should hold :

- At least 20 HCP between you and partner, *and*

- Four or more trumps, including at least two honours, *and*

- A shortage in partner's suit, preferably a singleton.

When To Double Their Suit Overcall At The Three-Level

As doubles above 2◊ give them a game if they succeed, you need to be very confident you will defeat them. For a penalty double at the three-level you should have six or more tricks between you and partner, including at least one trump trick. Partner should hold 1-2 tricks with 6-9 HCP and 2-3 tricks with 10-15 HCP. Add your own winners to this expectancy.

If you are highly likely to make a game, do not settle for a small penalty. Rather bid on to your best game. If you can make a game, you need at least 500 points from the double as compensation for the game missed.

When To Double Their Game Contracts

If they bid above your game, double if your side has more points. However, if they have bid to a game without interference, you normally do not double, even though you hope to defeat them. Points are not enough. If they have a singleton or a void, your expected winners might be ruffed. The best time to double their game is if they have barely enough for game (they had an invitational auction like 1♡ : 1NT, 2◊ : 2♡, 3♡ : 4♡) *and* you know they are in for a bad break in trumps. Double and collect big.

When To Double Their Slams

Almost never double, even if you know you can defeat them! You might collect an extra 50 or 100 *if* you beat them but they collect an extra 230 (or 640 if they redouble) if they make it. Even with Q-J-10-9 in trumps, just pass and be satisfied to defeat them. If you double, they might bid some other slam, such as 6NT, which you are unable to beat. What a disaster!

CHAPTER 13

PLANNING THE PLAY AS DECLARER IN NO-TRUMPS

YOUR BASIC APPROACH

In a no-trumps contract, your general plan as declarer should be :

● **Count how many instant winners you have without losing the lead.**

● **Determine how many more tricks you need to make your contract.**

● **Check to see which suit will give you the best chance of making those extra tricks needed.**

● **Play that suit, and do not be frightened to give up the lead once, or more often, if that is necessary to establish winners.**

Many players when they start playing hate to give up the lead early on, play their sure winners, and hope that all will be well at the end. One of the great challenges in bridge is that you are able to *plan your play*, often with great accuracy, because the dummy hand is revealed. The usual strategy of no-trumps play is : *first set up the extra tricks you need, later play your sure winning cards.*

Much of the time this approach will find your playing the partnership's longest combined suit. Take this hand, for example :

```
            NORTH
            ♠ 4 3
            ♡ J 3
            ◇ K Q J 10 9 7 2
            ♣ 10 2
WEST                  EAST
♠ Q J 10 9 7 6        ♠ 8 5
♡ 10 8 7             ♡ K 9 6 4 2
◇ A 3               ◇ 6
♣ Q 4               ♣ K 8 7 6 3
            SOUTH
            ♠ A K 2
            ♡ A Q 5
            ◇ 8 5 4
            ♣ A J 9 5
```

North opened 3◇ and South bid 3NT. West led the queen of spades and South won with the ace. There are 4 instant winners (AK, A and A). Five extra tricks are needed.

The suit that can provide those tricks is diamonds. Declarer should lead a diamond at trick two. If West does not take the ace, dummy will win the trick. Continue diamonds, forcing the ace out. Declarer can win any return and take the rest of the diamond winners, making ten tricks at least.

If South plays the instant winners before starting on the diamonds, declarer would fail, since the defenders can then take all their spade, heart and club winners before declarer can use the diamond winners.

It is not correct to say that you should *always* tackle the longest combined suit. *Play the suit which will provide the extra tricks you need.* In this next example, South opened 1NT and North raised to 3NT. West leads the jack of spades. Which suit should declarer play after winning the spade lead?

NORTH
- ♠ A Q 2
- ♡ 8 7
- ◊ K J 5 2
- ♣ A 8 7 3

WEST
- ♠ J 10 9 8 7
- ♡ A 6 5
- ◊ 8 6 4
- ♣ Q 5

EAST
- ♠ 5 4
- ♡ K 4 3 2
- ◊ Q 10 9 7
- ♣ J 10 9

SOUTH
- ♠ K 6 3
- ♡ Q J 10 9
- ◊ A 3
- ♣ K 6 4 2

Declarer can count seven instant winners (3 in spades, 2 in diamonds, 2 in clubs). Two extra tricks are needed. The longest combined suit is clubs, but if you play ♣A, ♣K and give up a club, that sets up only one extra winner (as long as clubs divide 3-2). As one extra trick is not enough, you must use the heart suit which can provide two extra tricks. The ♡Q would force out the ace or king. Later the ♡J would force out the other top honour. Then the ♡10 and ♡9 would be high. The correct play at trick two is to lead hearts.

It is important to know the general principles of play and which suit will produce the most tricks for you. However, one of declarer's greatest challenges is to know when to depart from normal strategy. Many declarers would go wrong on this deal where South opened 1NT and North raised to 3NT. How would you play as South in 3NT after a spade lead?

NORTH
- ♠ 3 2
- ♡ 8 7 6
- ◊ A K Q J
- ♣ K 9 8 5

WEST
- ♠ Q J 10 6 5 4
- ♡ A 3 2
- ◊ 10
- ♣ J 7 6

EAST
- ♠ 9 8 7
- ♡ K 5 4
- ◊ 9 8 4 3
- ♣ Q 10 4

SOUTH
- ♠ A K
- ♡ Q J 10 9
- ◊ 7 6 5 2
- ♣ A 3 2

With 8 instant winners (2 spades, 2 clubs and 4 diamonds), one extra trick is needed. The hearts can yield two tricks. Clubs can provide one extra trick if the suit splits 3-3. Even though hearts can give you two tricks for sure and the clubs at best one and then only on a favourable break, the correct play at trick two is clubs. Ace, king and a third club sets up dummy's last club as a winner.

Setting up hearts means losing the lead twice. South cannot afford that. By then the opponents would have set up and cashed their spades.

On the preceding deal, declarer could improve the play slightly. Before tackling clubs, South could play four rounds of diamonds, forcing the opponents to discard. Perhaps an opponent throws the wrong card. If one opponent started with four clubs and discards one, South makes the contract while playing clubs at once would have failed. It costs nothing to give the opposition a chance to make a mistake. After the diamonds, South should let the opponents win the first or second round of clubs. *If you have to lose a trick to set up winners, lose that trick as soon as convenient.*

That principle is at work on this hand :

NORTH
♠ J 8 7
♡ 6 5 4
♦ 6 5
♣ A 5 4 3 2

South opened 2NT and North raised to 3NT. West led the 10 of spades. How should South plan the play?

There are seven instant winners and declarer needs two more. The only suit which can provide the extra tricks is clubs but even then declarer needs to take care.

SOUTH
♠ A K Q
♡ A J 10
♦ A J 7 2
♣ K 7 6

It would be wrong to play the king of clubs followed by a club to the ace and then a third club. If clubs are 3-2, you will have two extra club winners in dummy but as dummy has no further *entry*, you will be unable to reach dummy to cash those winners.

Correct play is to cash the king of clubs and play a low club from both hands next. *Give up what you have to give up to set up extra tricks.* Win any return and play a club to the ace. Now you are in dummy and can cash the other two club winners.

OTHER GENERAL PRINCIPLES OF DECLARER PLAY

1. The hold-up play

If you have just one stopper in the suit led, say A-x-x opposite x-x, it is usually sensible not to win your ace until the third round. Your aim is to exhaust one opponent's cards in this suit so that if that opponent gains the lead later, he will be unable to return the suit led. You still win your ace but you simply win it later. *Do not use the hold-up play if there is some other suit which is even weaker than the suit led.* Better then to take your ace at once. If not, the opponents may switch to your weaker suit.

With K-x-x in hand opposite x-x in dummy, take your king at once if the suit is led and the ace is not played. You may not have another chance to win with the king. However, if the ace is played at trick one and the suit is returned, you should normally let the second round go, winning the king on the third round. This is a variation of the hold-up play. Again, grab the king if some other suit is even more dangerous for you.

The hold-up play is common at no-trumps. It is available in trumps play but rarely used. You can ruff if the opponents continue with their long suit.

2. Where to win the first trick

When you have a choice of winning the first trick in dummy or in your own hand, do not play a card until you have studied both hands and decided which suit you will play at trick two. Once you have made that decision it will often be clear where to win the first trick.

If you intend setting up a long suit, keep entries to the hand which has the long suit. Therefore win the first trick in the other hand. For example :

NORTH
♠ A 5 2
♡ 8 7 4
◇ Q 10 9 6 5
♣ 5 4

SOUTH
♠ K 6
♡ A K 5
◇ K J 7
♣ A J 9 8 2

South opened 1♣, North bid 1◇ and South rebid 3NT. West led the ♠Q. How should South plan the play?

Correct play is to win the first trick with the king of spades, not the ace. The suit to establish is diamonds. With five instant winners, you need to set up four more, all of which can come from the diamonds after the ace has been forced out. Therefore keep the ♠A as an entry to your long suit. At trick 2 lead the ◇K. If the opponents do not take it, continue with the ◇J. If the ace has still not been played, continue diamonds. Later cross to dummy with a spade to the ace and play the rest of the diamonds.

South could make three mistakes :

(1) By winning the first trick with the ace of spades. Then if the defenders do not take the ace of diamonds on the first two leads of diamonds (hold-up play by the defenders), declarer will be unable to return to dummy.

(2) By playing low on the first lead of spades (wrong use of hold-up play). South wins the second spade with the king but if the defenders again hold off with the ◇A until the third round (good defenders will), then declarer cannot cross to dummy as declarer is out of spades.

(3) By leading a low diamond to dummy's queen first. Suppose the opponents take the ◇A and play another spade. After winning the ♠A, you can play the ◇K and ◇J, but then you cannot return to dummy because you are out of diamonds. You have *blocked* the diamond suit which brings us to the next principle.

3. The High-Card-From-Shortage Rule

When you have winners in both hands, avoid blocking the suit by playing first the winners from the hand which is shorter in the suit. Thus, if dummy has three cards and you have only two, play the winner from your own hand first (you have the shortage), but if dummy has three cards and you have four, play the winners from dummy first (dummy has the shortage). See also Chapter 2, pages 35-36. A particular deal may require different treatment but the general rule is play the winners first from the shorter hand.

You	Dummy	
K 6	A Q 5	Play the king first. If in dummy, lead the 5 to the king.
A K Q 2	J 7	Play the jack first. If in hand, lead the 2 to the jack.
A J 7	K Q 5 4	Play ace first and jack next (high from shortage), then lead the 7 to dummy. If in dummy, lead 4 to the ace.

The same principle applies when you do not have winners but you are setting up winners by driving out the opposition's ace or the ace and king :

K 7	Q J 10 2	Play the king first. If in dummy, lead the 2 to the king.
K Q 5 4	J 10 6	Play the jack first, then the ten.
Q J 2	10 9 6 5	Play the queen first, the jack next.

4. The Highest-of-Equals Rule

It pays to be a deceptive declarer by not letting the defenders know which high cards you hold. Everybody can see dummy's cards but since they cannot see your cards, you can impede their task of working out where the missing high cards are. When you can win in hand with equally high cards, win with the highest of equal cards. Thus if you hold A-K and that suit is led, it will usually be more deceptive if you win with the ace.

Since it makes no difference to you with which card you win, you may as well make it harder for them. If you win with the king, one or both defenders can often tell that you hold the ace as well. If you win with the ace, they may not be sure whether you hold the king or whether their partner does.

Similarly, with A-K-J-10, if the suit is led and you can win with the jack or the ten, choose the jack. With A-Q-J-10 and you can win it with the queen, the jack or the ten, prefer to win with the queen.

5. Do not block your long suit

When playing a long suit, you will often need to keep the lead in the hand which has the long suit. With high cards in both hands, you may win a trick in the wrong hand if you have not taken care. This is a typical example :

You	Dummy	
9863	AKQ52	If you want dummy to win five tricks, you have to be careful that dummy can win the fourth round.

Some players would slip up and discover their mistake too late. If you play the 3 to the ace and cash the king and the queen you will find that the fourth round is won not in dummy but in your own hand. You have *blocked* the suit. Since the lead needs to stay in dummy, dummy must be able to win the fourth round of the suit. Therefore the 5 has to be a winner and it can be a winner only if you have retained the 3 in your own hand. To *unblock* the suit, play the 9, 8 and 6 under the A, K, Q.

6. How to count the missing cards

Once you gain experience you will want to count how many cards have gone in each suit and how many are still held by the opponents. At first, concentrate on just your longest combined suit, usually your trump suit, or on the two longest combined suits. Once you can count those correctly, you can extend your skill to all the suits.

Some players count out a suit this way : 'Four went on the first round and three have gone on the next round and dummy has two and I have two, so take all that away from 13 and there are still two missing.' This approach is not best since it requires about five steps and an error at any stage will mean you have the wrong answer. Also your concentration will wane if you have to keep doing so many sums.

A more efficient method is to work out as soon as dummy appears how many cards the opponents hold in your two longest suits. If dummy has 3 and you have 5, you know that they started with 5. Then you need concentrate only on *the cards that they play* without worrying about how many have gone and how many you have left. If they began with 5 and they play one each on the first round, they have 3 left, 5 minus 2, one simple step. If they both follow to the next lead, there is only one left (3 minus 2).

If dummy started with 6 and you started with 1, then the opponents began with 6. If they follow to the first lead, they must have 4 left. If they both follow to the second lead, there must still be two out. If one opponent shows out on the third round of the suit, the other opponent still has one card left in that suit. You can also deduce that the missing cards originally divided 4-2.

7. How to work out where the missing high cards are located

An excellent habit to develop is to count dummy's HCP and add your own as soon as dummy appears. By deducting from 40 (the total HCP in the pack) you know how many HCP the other two players have between them. If there has been any opposition bidding, you can often place the missing high cards. These are some useful principles :

Assume that a player who has opened has at least 11-12 HCP.

Assume that a player who has not opened has less than 12 HCP.

If one opponent opened and the other did not respond, assume that the responder has less than 6 HCP.

Assume that a one-level overcaller has at least 7-8 HCP and a two-level overcaller at least 9-10 HCP.

Assume that a player who made a takeout double has at least 11-12 HCP.

NOTE : Sections 2 to 7 above apply equally when playing in a trump contract, covered in Chapter 14.

CHAPTER 14

PLANNING THE PLAY AS DECLARER IN TRUMP CONTRACTS

The general plan in no-trumps is to count your winners and if not enough, play the suit which will bring in the extra tricks needed.

In a trump contract, it is better to count your losers and with more losers than you can afford, plan a way to eliminate some of those losers. When counting losers, count them from your own hand but take into account high cards in dummy which can cover your losers.

You	Dummy	
A K 6	8 7 2	You have one loser. Dummy cannot cover that loser.
A K 6	Q 7 2	You have one loser. Dummy's Q covers that loser.
9 8 3	K Q J 4	You have three losers. Dummy can cover two losers.

When you do not have too many losers, it is usually best to draw trumps at once. When you have more losers than you can afford, the most common ways of eliminating them are to *ruff losers in dummy* OR *discard losers on extra winners in dummy*.

Ruffing losers in dummy

The most common problem in a trump contract is whether to play trumps at once or whether to delay trumps. If you need to ruff losers in dummy, do not draw so many rounds of trumps that dummy is left without enough trumps to ruff those losers.

NORTH
♠ 3
♡ 10 9
♢ 8 6 5 3 2
♣ J 7 5 4 3

SOUTH
♠ A 6 5
♡ A K Q J 5 4
♢ A K
♣ 8 2

South opened 2♡ and North bid 2NT. South rebid 3♡ and North raised to 4♡. West leads the ♠J. Plan South's play.

South can count 4 losers (2 in spades, 2 in clubs). The spade losers can be eliminated by ruffing them in dummy. It would be a serious error to play trumps first. Dummy would be unable to ruff both spade losers.

Correct play is to win the ♠A and play back a spade, ruffing it in dummy. A diamond to the ace is followed by another spade, again ruffing it in dummy. Now declarer has only two losers instead of four.

NORTH
♠ J 8 2
♡ 7 6
◇ K Q
♣ 8 7 6 5 4 3

South opened 1♠, North bid 1NT, South jumped to 3♡ (jump-shift game force) and North's 4♠ ended the bidding. Plan the play after West leads a diamond.

SOUTH
♠ K Q 10 9 5
♡ A K 5 4
◇ A J
♣ Q 2

Win the diamond in dummy, cash the ♡A, ♡K and ruff a heart with dummy's ♠8. A diamond to the ace allows South to lead the fourth heart, ruffing with the ♠J. From here you should lose no more than two clubs and the ♠A.

South began with 5 losers (2 clubs, 2 hearts, 1 spade), but dummy's shortage in hearts allowed two losers to be eliminated by ruffing.

Even though declarer needed only two trumps in dummy for the two heart ruffs, it would have been an error to lead even one round of trumps. That would have given the defenders the opportunity to play a second round of trumps, reducing dummy to one trump, not enough to ruff two losers.

Note that the third heart was ruffed with the *eight* of trumps, not the 2. *Ruff as high as you can afford* is a sound guide. If an opponent could overruff dummy, it could only be with the ace of trumps, an inevitable loser. For the same reason, the fourth heart was ruffed with the jack of spades.

NORTH
♠ Q 9 3
♡ 8 7 6 2
◇ Q 5
♣ A 8 5 4

South : 1♠, North : 1NT, South : 3♠, North : 4♠. How would you play after West leads a heart?

With 4 losers (3 diamonds, 1 club), you plan to ruff the third diamond in dummy. You need only one ruff but if you play two rounds of trumps and an opponent has a trump left, you may find that when you lose the lead in diamonds, that opponent plays the trump to draw dummy's last trump.

SOUTH
♠ A K J 10 5 4
♡ A K
◇ 8 7 4
♣ J 3

Correct is to win ♡A and lead diamonds at once. Continue diamonds at each opportunity and ruff the third diamond high in dummy. Only then draw trumps.

You do not need any special reason to draw trumps. Drawing trumps is the normal process. You do need a sound reason to delay drawing trumps.

NORTH
♠ J 9 7
♡ A K Q 4
◇ Q 10 4
♣ 8 7 2

North : 1NT, South : 3♠, North : 4♠. How would you play if West leads (a) a heart? (b) a club?

On a heart lead, win and start trumps at once. If they win and shift to a club, take your ace and play two more trumps, ending in dummy. Then cash two top hearts and discard two club losers.

SOUTH
♠ K Q 10 8 6
♡ 3
◇ K J 9 3
♣ A 5 4

On a club lead, you must not touch trumps yet. You have four immediate losers. Win ♣A and play three rounds of hearts at once, discarding your two club losers. Then shift to the trumps and you should lose just two aces.

Further examples of discarding losers on dummy's winners can be found on pages 56-57, Deals 9, 10 and 12. Sometimes in order to have extra tricks in dummy for discards you need to knock out an enemy high card first.

NORTH
♠ J 10 9 4
♡ 7 6 5
◇ K Q 10 8
♣ 6 3

SOUTH
♠ A K Q 6 3
♡ A K 3
◇ J 6 5
♣ Q 4

South : 1♠, North : 2♠, South : 4♠. How would you play after West leads the queen of hearts?

You can count 4 losers (2 clubs, 1 diamond and 1 heart). Dummy has no extra winners yet but an extra winner can be established by knocking out the ace of diamonds because dummy has an extra card in diamonds.

Correct is to win the lead with the ♡A, draw trumps and then lead the ◇J. Keep playing diamonds until they take the ace. When you regain the lead, continue the diamonds and discard the heart loser on the fourth diamond.

Sometimes you may have to knock out their ace before you tackle trumps.

NORTH
♠ J 10 9 4
♡ K 6 5
◇ K Q 8
♣ Q 6 3

SOUTH
♠ K Q 8 6 3
♡ A 3 2
◇ J 6
♣ K J 10

South : 1♠, North : 3♠, South : 4♠. How would you play after West leads the queen of hearts?

You are sure to lose three aces and cannot afford to lose a heart as well. It would be an error to lead trumps at once. The opponents could win the ♠A and lead a second heart. Now you are faced with a heart loser as well as the three aces to be lost.

Correct is to win the lead with the ♡A and lead the ◇J at once. If they duck this, lead another diamond. If they win this and lead a second heart, win the ♡K and pitch your heart loser on the third diamond.

Note that it was important on the hand above to win the opening lead with the ace in hand. If the opponents do not take the first diamond, you need the king of hearts in dummy as a later entry to the diamonds.

Many declarers would go wrong on this deal :

NORTH
♠ K 8 7
♡ 8 3 2
◇ A 6
♣ A J 7 6 3

SOUTH
♠ A Q J 10 3
♡ 6 5 4
◇ K Q 5
♣ 4 2

North : 1NT, South : 3♠, North : 4♠. Luckily a heart is not led. How would you play after West leads a club?

You have three heart losers and a club to lose, too. On the surface there is nothing to be ruffed in dummy and dummy has no extra winners for discards. However South's extra diamond winner can create a shortage in dummy.

Win the ♣A, play ◇A, ◇K and ◇Q, discarding a heart from dummy. Then lead a heart. Keep leading hearts at each opportunity until dummy is void. Then ruff your third heart in dummy. After that, trumps can be drawn.

Keep count of the missing trumps

It is important to keep an accurate count of the trumps and to be aware of how many are left against you. How to keep track of the trumps was discussed on page 123.

When to draw the last trump

If you are drawing trumps and one trump is still missing, draw the last trump if it is lower than yours. If the last trump is higher than yours, it is often best to leave the last trump out.

If it is lower than yours, it is a good idea to remove it. Otherwise, they may score a trick with that lower trump by ruffing one of your winners.

If it is higher than yours, it is usually sensible to leave it out. It is a trick for the opponents anyway and removing it costs you one or two trumps and loses the lead. If they do ruff one of your winners later, it is with a trump that you were bound to lose. Your remaining trumps will then be high.

In one situation it is important to remove the last trump even though theirs is higher than yours. If dummy has a long, strong suit but no other entries, you cannot afford to leave a trump out before you run this suit. Otherwise, they may be able to ruff and prevent your using all of dummy's winners.

Ruff your losers in the shorter trump hand

Normally you do not benefit by ruffing cards in your own hand if you have more trumps than dummy. Plan to ruff losers in the shorter trump hand.

If you find yourself ruffing in the longer trump hand, make sure you have a sound reason. The fallacy of ruffing with the longer trumps can be seen in a case like this. If hearts are trumps, how many winners does West have?

WEST	EAST	
♡ A K Q J 10 9	♡ 8 7 6	By simply leading out the trumps, West has six winners.

How many tricks will West have if West ruffs with the 9 of hearts? Still 6 : one trick by ruffing and five top winners. What if West ruffs with the 9 and again with the 10? Still 6 winners in total : two ruffs and four top winners. Ruffing with the long trumps does not normally produce any extra winners.

By contrast if West can arrange to ruff something in dummy, that is an extra trick : one ruff in the East hand plus the six that West always had. If West can ruff twice in the East hand, there would be a total of eight tricks and if West could manage to ruff three times with the East trumps, West would score nine tricks, making each of the trump winners separately.

Ruffing in the long trump hand usually does not gain. Ruffing in the shorter trump hand does gain.

CHAPTER 15

WINNING STRATEGY
FOR THE DEFENDERS

Defending well is much more difficult than playing well as declarer. Declarer has the benefit of seeing both hands, the total assets. The defenders do not. As a consequence, the defenders use a system of leads, signals and plays designed to help them deduce what partner holds.

It is vital to be aware of the bidding and of the number of tricks you need to defeat the contract. If declarer is in 4♠, declarer's contract is to win ten tricks or more. It is useful to consider that the defenders have their contract, too, and that is to win four tricks or more. It would therefore be foolish to embark on a defence that can yield only two tricks at best.

There are a number of guides designed to help the defenders. They are useful provided you treat them merely as guides and not as unbreakable rules. If you can see that following one of these guides will help declarer and will not help you, then by all means ignore the guide.

Paying attention to the bidding, counting the cards that have gone and noting the number of tricks still needed to defeat the contract are far more important than any of these guides. Nevertheless the guides are helpful when you have no clear-cut direction to take.

1. Second hand usually plays low.

2. Third hand usually plays high.

3. It is often best to return your partner's lead.

4. Do not cover an honour with an honour unless it builds up an extra trick for you or may build up a trick for your partner.

Second hand low

'Second hand plays low' is often quoted together with 'third hand plays high'. The difference between playing second to a trick or third to a trick is that when you are the second hand, your partner still has to play to the trick. Partner may be able to play a card high enough to beat the cards played by declarer and dummy and prevent declarer from winning the trick.

However, it is sensible to play high in second position if you can win the trick and this is the trick that will defeat the contract. You might also win the trick in second seat if you know that partner cannot possibly win it. For example, if declarer plays the king and you have the ace, you should normally take your ace. It is clear that partner will not be able to beat the king. It also makes sense to play high and win in second position if by playing low you may not score a trick at all.

	Dummy	If declarer leads a low card from hand towards
	Q 5	dummy's queen, West should take the king.
West		Otherwise West may not take a trick with the king
K 6		at all.

	Dummy	Declarer leads low towards dummy's king. If you
	K 7 5 4	need only one trick to defeat the contract, take
West		your ace. If you need more than one trick or you
A 9 2		are sure the ace will make later, play low. If
		declarer might be leading a singleton, grab the ace.

The main purpose of playing 'second hand low' is to make sure that your honours capture the honours of the opponent sitting on your right.

	Dummy	If declarer leads a low card towards dummy's
	Q 5 3	queen, West should play low. If West plays the
West		ace, declarer scores two tricks, the queen and the
A 6 2		king. If West plays second hand low, the queen in
	Declarer	dummy wins but West has the ace left to capture
	K 8 7	declarer's king. Declarer makes one trick only.

There is also a deceptive element in playing 'second hand low'. Suppose declarer leads the 2 from the 7 4 2 in dummy and you are second to play with A 9 5. It might look harmless to grab your ace. After all dummy has no high card. However, what if declarer holds K J? If you play your ace, declarer scores a trick with the king. If you play low, declarer might misguess and play the jack. That would give declarer no tricks, but only if you have played 'second hand low'.

Third hand high

If you are third to play on a trick, partner has already played and if partner's card cannot win the trick, you are the only one who can win the trick for your side. Even if you cannot win the trick, it is right to play high in third position in order to promote high cards in partner's hand.

	Dummy		West leads the 2. East should play the king.
	7 6 5		If East plays the 3 or the 9, South wins the
West		**East**	10 now and the ace later, two tricks. If East
Q J 4 2		K 9 3	plays the king, declarer makes only one trick.
	Declarer		Although the king loses to the ace, East has
	A 10 8		promoted West's queen and jack to winners.

Dummy	
10 6 5	
West	**East**
A J 7 4 2	K 9 3
Declarer	
Q 8	

In a no-trumps contract West leads the 4. If East plays the 9 or the 3, South can win an undeserved trick with the queen. If East plays the king (third hand high) and continues the suit, South wins no tricks in the suit and West can take four more tricks in the suit.

There are certain situations where it is wrong to play third hand high. If dummy has only low cards, third hand high will usually be right, but if dummy has the king, queen or jack and you have a higher honour and a lower honour, it usually works out best to play your lower honour.

Dummy	
Q 6 5	
West	**East**
K 10 8 4 2	A J 3
Declarer	
9 7	

West leads the 4 and dummy plays low. East does better by playing the jack, not the ace. The ace will win the trick but if the ace is played, the queen becomes a winner on the third round. By playing the jack, East stops declarer making any trick in the suit.

Dummy	
A J 7	
West	**East**
Q 6 4 2	K 10 3
Declarer	
9 8 5	

West leads the 2 and dummy plays low. East could play the king but playing the 10 holds South to one trick in the suit. Playing the king allows declarer to score two tricks by finessing the jack later. If South has the queen, East might still capture the jack later.

Third hand high is also not best when it sets up winners for declarer without producing any winners for the defence.

Dummy	
Q J 10 9 7	
West	**East**
8 4	K 6 3 2
Declarer	
A 5	

West leads the 8 and dummy plays the queen (or jack or 10 or 9). East should play low, not the king. The king would lose to the ace *and all dummy's cards would now be winners*. As the 8 lead marks South with the ace, East cannot win by playing the king.

Third hand does not play the highest card if the trick can be won with a cheaper card. *A defender wins with the cheapest card possible.* If you hold A-K-Q-4-2 as a defender in third position, win with the queen. Then partner will know you also hold the ace and king. Partner can also deduce that you do not hold the jack. If you held A-K-Q-J, you would have won with the jack, your cheapest winning card.

From this it follows that *if third hand wins with a high card, this denies holding the next lower card.* If you win with the king, you do not have the queen, if you win with the ace, you do not hold the king.

The same applies if you are playing third hand high with equally high cards. Suppose you hold K-Q-J. Partner leads low and dummy plays low. You should play the jack, the cheapest of equally high cards. This play will often help partner work out the location of the high cards in a suit.

In third seat play the cheapest of equally high cards. It follows that when third hand plays high, the card played denies the next cheaper card. When playing third hand high, the play of the 10 denies the 9, the play of the jack denies the 10, the play of the queen denies the jack, and so on.

	Dummy	
	10 5 4	
West		**East**
Q 7 6 3 2		J 9
	Declarer	
	A K 8	

West leads the 3, dummy plays low, East plays the 9 and South wins the ace. West knows East has the jack (else South would have won with the jack), that South has the king (East would play the king from K-J) and that South has the 8 (the 9 denied the 8)!

Return partner's lead

This is a good guide since partner has usually a sound reason for selecting a particular lead. In no-trumps it is likely to be partner's best suit and it pays you to force out any stoppers declarer has. In a trump contract it might be a singleton lead and so if you return the lead, partner can score a ruff.

You should always consider whether returning partner's lead will help to defeat their contract. If you have a better suit of your own, it may be correct to switch or if you can see that returning partner's lead is futile, you might decide to shift to another suit which might defeat the contract.

♠ A 6 5
♡ 7 4
♢ A K Q 8 3 2
♣ A 4

♠ K 3
♡ Q J 10 3
♢ 9 7 6
♣ J 10 5 3

North 1♢, South : 1NT, North : 3NT. West leads the jack of spades, low from dummy. How should East plan the defence?

The jack lead marks South with the ♠ Q. As partner's card will not win the trick, East should play the king to win. What next?

Many players would return a spade but you can see that this would be futile. With the ♠Q, South has 9 tricks now available.

East can see declarer can win the ♠ Q, the ♠ A, the ♣ A and six diamonds as soon as South gains the lead. East should switch to the queen of hearts and if South has a hand like ♠ Q 7 4 ♡ K 9 2 ♢ J 5 4 ♣ Q 9 8 7, the defence can win four heart tricks in addition to the ♠K. One down.

When you do decide to switch to a new suit, it is usually best not to switch to a suit where dummy has length or where declarer is known to have length.

Cover an honour with an honour

When declarer leads an honour card from hand or declarer leads an honour card from dummy, second player should often play a higher honour even though your honour card may not win the trick. By covering the honour card you may be able to build up an extra trick for your side.

Take a pack of cards and arrange the suits as below.

Dummy
♠ A J 4 2
♡ A J 4 2
◊ A 5 4 2
♣ A 5 4 2

West	East
♠ K 10 9	♠ 7 6 5
♡ K 6 3	♡ 10 9 8
◊ K 6 3	◊ 10 9 8
♣ K 6 3	♣ 9 8 7

Declarer
♠ Q 8 3
♡ Q 7 5
◊ Q J 7
♣ Q J 10

In each case declarer leads the queen from hand. through West towards dummy. Should West play the king or play low?

What if declarer leads a low card from hand through West towards dummy? Should West play the king or play low?

The common theme in spades, hearts and diamonds is that if South leads the queen, you must cover with the king *promoting* a trick for the ten. You can see the point in covering in the spade suit because you have the ♠10, but it is equally true in the heart and diamond suits when East has the ten.

On the other hand if South leads a low card you should also play low, retaining your king to axe South's queen. *The purpose of an honour card is to kill opponent's honours.*

In the club suit, covering the queen with the king gains nothing as South has the jack and ten, but it loses nothing either.

There are situations where it is wrong to cover an honour with an honour. The main guide is that you should cover an honour card led by declarer or from dummy *if it can benefit your side,* by promoting a trick for you or possibly promoting one for your partner.

Dummy
J 6

West	East
K 9 5	Q 4

Declarer
A 10 8 7 3 2

If the jack is led from dummy and East plays low, declarer will play low, losing to West's king. Declarer will lose just one trick. If East covers the jack with the queen, the defenders come to two tricks. If South takes the queen with the ace, West has K-9 over declarer's 10-8. Covering promoted the 9.

Dummy
Q 6

West	East
A	K J 4

Declarer
10 9 8 7 5 3 2

Declarer seems destined to lose three tricks but a canny declarer will set a trap that only the best defenders will avoid. Declarer should cross to dummy and lead the queen. If East covers with the king, three losers become two as the bare ace falls on the king.

Covering the queen with the king here is a blind spot. Imagine that declarer does have A-10-9-x-x-x or similar. If East covers, how many tricks will East take? One only. And how many tricks if East does not cover the queen? Also one. As covering cannot gain, East may as well play low. A sound principle in this area is : *Do not cover an honour with an honour if partner is known to be short in the suit.* If East can tell that West has only a singleton or a doubleton, it will not pay to cover.

Beware when giving declarer a ruff

Be careful when leading a suit that you do not give ruffs that will provide declarer with extra tricks. For example, it is usually not a good idea to lead a suit which can be ruffed in dummy. This is usually declarer's shorter trump holding and this ruff may give declarer an extra trick.

It is not automatically wrong to give declarer a ruff. It may be your safest exit or you may be able to reduce declarer's trump holding and cause declarer to lose control of the trump suit. Just be cautious and make sure that there is nothing better offering.

In particular, when dummy has a long, strong suit which will provide discards for declarer, you must grab your tricks in the other suits before declarer has time to discard the losers in those suits. With a long suit in dummy, declarer's plan will be to draw trumps and run the long suit. Giving declarer a ruff does nothing to hinder that plan. The sight of a long suit in dummy means that the defence should usually attack one of the other suits.

Sometimes your best defence is to lead trumps. If the bidding indicates that dummy has useful ruffing values (for example, when declarer bids two suits and dummy supports declarer's second suit), an opening trump lead may be best. On other occasions it may become obvious when dummy appears or as the play progresses that declarer plans to use dummy's trumps to ruff losers. You may be able to frustrate declarer's plans or at least minimise the ruffs in dummy by switching to trumps, thus reducing dummy's trumping power.

Signals and discards

If partner leads a suit and you are not trying to win the trick, you can signal to partner whether you wish to have the suit continued. Use these rules :

1. Higher card followed by lower card (high-low signal) says 'Please continue with a third round of this suit'. For example, 7 then 4 = 'come on signal'.

2. Lower card followed by a higher card, for example 7 then 9, says 'Please do *not* continue this suit. Switch to some other suit.'

3. If unable to make a complete two-card signal, a high card says 'Please continue'. Usually a 6 or higher is enough to make partner sit up and take notice. Playing your lowest possible card = 'Please switch now'.

4. When signalling partner to continue a suit, play the highest card you can afford. If you want to signal high with Q 10 9 8 3, signal with the 10. If you can afford the 8, you can afford the 9 and likewise you can afford the 10.

5. When discarding, you can also signal to partner. A high discard says 'Please play this suit'. Discarding the lowest card in a suit says 'Please do *not* play this suit. Try something else.' It is usually more efficient to discard lowest in the suits you do not want rather than squander a high card in the suit you do want partner to play. Above all, do not discard a card that could become a winner. High cards are meant to win tricks. Do not waste them.

Keep length with dummy when choosing your discards

When forced to make a discard, avoid throwing from a 4-card or 5-card suit where dummy has four or more cards in the same suit if it is possible for one of your cards to win a trick. Keep the same length as dummy has. Likewise do not discard from length in a suit if declarer is known to have length in that suit. Keep length with declarer.

Dummy		Even though East's cards seem useless, it
A K 6 2		could be an error to throw even one away.
	East	East has the same length as dummy and the 8
	8 5 4 3	is enough to beat dummy's 6.

Imagine that South holds Q 9 and West J 10 7. Declarer is entitled to win three tricks with the Q, K and A but if East discards a card from this suit, declarer will win an extra trick. After the Q, K and A, neither defender will have a card left in the suit and the 6 will have become a winner.

Lead through strength, lead up to weakness

This is a reasonable guide most of the time. 'Lead through strength' means that if dummy is *on your left*, choose to lead a strong suit in dummy, a suit with one or two honours, rather than a suit where dummy has no honours at all. When leading one of dummy's strong suits, choose a *short* suit, no longer than three cards. Otherwise you may well be helping declarer establish dummy's long suit.

'Lead up to weakness' means that if dummy is *on your right*, prefer to lead a suit in which dummy has no honour card. Again be wary of leading a suit where dummy has length. Attack dummy's two- or three-card suits.

Unblocking under partner's lead

If partner leads an honour and you hold ace-doubleton or king-doubleton, you should play your honour in order to 'unblock' the suit, to get out of partner's way. This is usually safe as partner's honour card lead will be from a sequence. This unblocking applies in no-trumps and trump contracts.

Dummy		If West leads the queen, East should play
7 6 2		the king to unblock. If West leads the jack or
	East	the 10, East would play the king anyway as
	K 3	third-hand-high.

	Dummy		When West leads the king, East should play
	7 6 2		the ace. If East plays low, the defence takes
West		**East**	only two tricks in the suit immediately. West
K Q J 9 8		A 5	needs an entry to cash the other winners. If
	Declarer		East plays the ace and returns the suit, the
	10 4 3		defence can come to all their tricks at once.

EXERCISES

1. NORTH
♠ A K 5
♡ K 7 4
♢ J 10 7 2
♣ 7 6 2

EAST
♠ 6 4 3
♡ A 9 2
♢ K 4 3
♣ A 8 4 3

The bidding :

SOUTH NORTH
1NT 3NT

West leads the 8 of spades won by the ace in dummy.

Which card should East play if declarer then leads each of the following cards :

(a) ♡4? (b) ♡K? (c) ♢J? (d) ♣2?

2. **NORTH**
♠ K J 5
♡ A J
♢ K 10 9 8 4
♣ 9 6 2

WEST
♠ A 6 2
♡ K 7 4
♢ Q 7
♣ K Q J 10 3

The bidding :

SOUTH NORTH
1NT 3NT

West leads the king of clubs and queen of clubs which win. Declarer wins trick 3 with the ace of clubs..

Which card should West play if declarer then leads each of the following cards :

(a) ♠4? (b) ♡2? (c) ♡Q? (d) ♢J?

3. Dummy
♢ 10 7 2

East
♢ ?

SOUTH NORTH
1NT 3NT

West leads the 4 of diamonds, dummy playing the 2. Which diamond should East play from each of the following holdings?

(a) ♢ A K 6? (b) ♢ K J 6? (c) ♢ K Q 6? (d) ♢ J 9 6? (e) ♢ Q J 9 8?

4. Dummy
♠ Q 7 4

East
♠ ?

SOUTH NORTH
1NT 3NT

West leads the 3 of spades, dummy playing the 4. Which spade should East play from each of the following holdings?

(a) ♠ A K 6? (b) ♠ A K J? (c) ♠ A J 6? (d) ♠ K J 10 9? (e) ♠ K 10 6?

5. Dummy
♡ J 7 4

East
♡ ?

SOUTH	NORTH
1♠	3♠
4♠	Pass

West leads the king of hearts, dummy playing the 4. Which heart should East play from each of the following holdings?

(a) ♡A 9 6 2?   (b) ♡8 6 5 2?   (c) ♡A 3?   (d) ♡A Q 9 8 2?   (e) ♡A 5 3 2?

6. NORTH
♠ A K 5
♡ 9 7 4
◊ K Q 10 2
♣ Q 6 2

EAST
♠ 8 7 4 3 2
♡ 8 6 3 2
◊ - - -
♣ A K J 10

The bidding :

SOUTH	NORTH
1NT	3NT

West leads the 4 of diamonds which does not surprise you in the least. Dummy plays ◊2.

Which card should East discard? What do you want West to do if West comes on lead?

7.   **Dummy**
♣ K 4 2

West
♣ J 7 6 5 3

SOUTH	NORTH
1NT	3NT

You, West, lead the 5 of clubs, the 2 is played from dummy, partner plays the 9 and declarer wins with the ace. What is the layout of this suit? Can you tell . . .

(a) Who has the queen?   (b) Who has the 8?   (c) Who has the 10?

8.   **Dummy**
♡ 10 6 4

West
♡ Q 8 5 3 2

SOUTH	NORTH	
1NT	2♣ (1)	(1) Stayman Convention
2◊ (2)	3NT	(2) No 4-card major

You, West, lead the 3 of hearts, the 4 is played from dummy, partner plays the jack and declarer wins with the ace. What is the layout of this suit? Can you tell . . .

(a) Who has the king?   (b) Who has the 9?   (c) Who has the 7?

9. Partner has led a low card, dummy has only low cards and you have won the trick with your ace. You intend to return partner's suit. Which card would you lead back from each of these original holdings?
(a) A 8 2   (b) A 8 4 2   (c) A 8 6 4 2   (d) A Q 2   (e) A J 10 2

136

APPENDIX 1 : THE STAYMAN CONVENTION

All players of experience know and understand the Stayman Convention, a response of 2♣ to a 1NT opening. The Stayman 2♣ is designed to locate the best game contract with a 4-4 fit in a major suit in preference to no-trumps. After playing for some time, you will want to include Stayman in your system, since Stayman is part and parcel of all standard systems.

The 2♣ response to 1NT asks partner, 'Do you have a 4-card major?' If opener has a major, opener bids it. The negative reply, denying a 4-card major, is 2◊. If opener has two 4-card majors, bid 2♡ (4-card suits up-the-line).

WHEN TO USE STAYMAN

Use the 2♣ reply to 1NT when you hold :

● Enough points to invite a game, *and*

● One 4-card major or both majors, 4-4, 5-4 or 5-5. With a 5-5, if you bid 1NT : 3♠ you may end in a 5-3 spade fit with a 5-4 fit in hearts available. Using Stayman will locate the 5-4 fit if it exists.

REPLIES TO 2♣ STAYMAN

2◊ = No major suit

2♡ = 4 hearts (may have spades also)

2♠ = 4 spades (will not have four hearts)

AFTER OPENER'S REPLY TO STAYMAN

A new suit by responder is a 5-card suit and a jump-bid is forcing to game (e.g., 1NT : 2♣, 2◊ : 3♠ would show five spades and enough for game). If opener has bid one major, a bid of no-trumps by responder would show that responder had four cards in the other major. Responder's rebid of 2NT invites game (like 1NT : 2NT immediately). Raising opener's major suit to the 3-level likewise invites game and shows support of opener's major.

STAYMAN WITH WEAK RESPONDING HANDS

When responder bids 2♣ over 1NT and rebids 3♣ over opener's answer, responder is showing 6 or more clubs and a very weak hand (not enough for a game). Opener is expected to pass. Responder's rebid of 2-in-a-major is also a weak rebid showing a 5-card suit. Opener would normally pass but may raise the major with 3-card support and a maximum 1NT opening.

STAYMAN IN RESPONSE TO A 2NT OPENING

2NT : 3♣ operates like 1NT : 2♣, except that opener's replies are at the 3-level. To use Stayman over 2NT, responder should have enough strength for game and either one 4-card major or both majors. A new suit rebid by responder after the reply to Stayman would be at least a 5-card suit and would be forcing.

APPENDIX 2 : OPENING LEADS — THE SUIT TO LEAD

(1) AGAINST NO-TRUMP CONTRACTS :

Under normal circumstances, the best strategy is to lead your longest suit and both defenders continue with that suit at every opportunity unless from the preceding play it has become clearly futile to pursue that suit.

- Lead your own longest suit, *but*
- Prefer to lead a long suit bid by partner, *and*
- Avoid leading a suit which has been genuinely bid by the opponents.

Where partner has not bid a suit and your long suit has been bid by the opponents, choose another long suit if you have one, but if not, be prepared to lead even a 3-card suit. When faced with this decision to lead a short suit, prefer a major to a minor, longer to shorter and stronger to weaker.

(2) AGAINST TRUMP CONTRACTS :

It is no longer attractive to lead your long suit as declarer or dummy is likely to ruff this suit after one or two rounds. Prefer one of these highly attractive leads :

- A suit headed by a solid sequence, such as K-Q-J, Q-J-10, J-10-9, etc.
- A suit headed by A-K-Q or A-K, *or*
- A singleton, *or*
- A suit bid by partner.

If none of these attractive leads exists, avoid these dreadful leads :

- A suit headed by the ace without the king as well, *or*
- Doubleton honours, such as K-x, Q-x, J-x, *or*
- A singleton trump, *or*
- A suit bid by the opposition.

If you still have more than one suit left after eliminating the terrible leads :

- Lead a suit with two honours rather than a suit with just one honour.
- Lead a doubleton rather than a suit with just one honour.
- Lead a suit with no honours. A lead from 3 or 4 rags is often safer than one from a broken suit like K-J-x or a suit with only one honour.

A trump lead is reasonable from two or three worthless trumps if there is no evidence from the bidding that dummy holds a long suit.

If dummy is known to hold a long suit, lead an unbid suit. If you have just one honour card in the possible suits to lead, prefer a suit with the king to a suit with the queen; prefer a suit with the queen to a suit with the jack; prefer a suit with the jack to a suit with just the ace.

If you hold four or more trumps, lead your longest suit outside trumps to try to force declarer to ruff and so reduce declarer's trump length.

APPENDIX 3 : OPENING LEADS — THE CARD TO LEAD

The basic rules are :

● Top from a doubleton.

● From three cards : bottom with an honour — middle with no honour — top of two or three touching cards headed by an honour.

● From four or more cards, fourth-highest but lead top from solid sequences or near sequences and top of the touching honours when holding three honours.

In the list below, the card to lead is the same whether you are leading partner's suit or your own. The lead is the same for a trump contract or for no-trumps except for those with an asterisk.

Holding	Lead	Holding	Lead	Holding	Lead
9 5	9	Q J 10 2	Q	A K	K
9 5 3	5	Q J 9 2	Q	A 6	A
9 6 5 3 2	3	Q J 8 2	2	A K Q	A
10 9	10	Q 10 9 8	10	A K J	A
10 6	10	Q 10 8 3	3	A K 3	A
10 9 3	10	Q 9 8 7 6	7	A 9 3**	A
10 6 3	3	Q 8 6 5 2	5	A K Q 3	A
10 6 3 2	2	K Q	K	A K J 3	A
10 9 8 3	10	K 2	K	A K 6 3*	A
10 9 7 3	10	K Q 5	K	A Q J 3***	A
10 9 6 3	3	K J 10	J	A Q 6 3*	A
J 10	J	K J 5	5	A J 10 3***	A
J 5	J	K 10 9	10	A J 6 3*	A
J 10 6	J	K 10 5	5	A 10 9 8***	A
J 5 2	2	K 7 5	5	A 10 5 2*	A
J 5 4 2	2	K Q J 2	K	A 9 8 7*	A
J 9 8 7 6	7	K Q 10 2	K	A 9 6 3*	A
J 7 5 4 2	4	K Q 9 2*	K	A K J 4 2	A
J 10 9 4	J	K J 10 2	J	A K 7 4 2*	A
J 10 8 4	J	K J 9 2	2	A Q J 4 2***	A
J 10 7 4	4	K 10 9 8	10	A Q 10 9 2***	A
Q J	Q	K 10 8 4	4	A Q 10 4 2*	A
Q 4	Q	K Q J 6 3	K	A Q 6 4 2*	A
Q J 4	Q	K Q 10 6 3	K	A J 10 5 3***	A
Q 10 9	10	K Q 7 6 3*	K	A J 8 5 3*	A
Q 10 4	4	K 9 8 7 3	7	A 10 9 8 3***	A
Q 6 4	4	K 8 6 4 3	4	A 10 8 5 3*	A

*Lead fourth-highest against no-trumps   **Lead bottom against no-trumps
***Lead the top of the touching honours against no-trumps, e.g., Q from AQJxx, J from AJ10xx, 10 from A109, A1098 or AQ109x, and so on.

APPENDIX 4 : ETHICS AND ETIQUETTE

Bridge enjoys immense popularity partly because of the high standards of ethics and etiquette which are observed by the players who are expected to conduct themselves in a highly civilised manner. Violations of proper etiquette are quite common from inexperienced players, either through ignorance or inadvertence. A well-mannered opponent who is the victim of a violation by such a novice player will, if comment is considered necessary, be at pains to make it clear that the comment is intended to be helpful and will never make a newcomer feel ill-at-ease.

Bridge is an extremely ethical game. All good players strive to ensure that their bridge ethics are impeccable and no more serious charge, other than outright cheating, can be made than to accuse a player of bad ethics. Unlike poker in which all sorts of mannerisms, misleading statements and bluff tactics are part and parcel of the game, bridge is played with a 'pokerface'! Beginners are, of course, excused for their lapses and in social games nobody minds very much, but in serious competition your bridge demeanour must be beyond reproach.

When you are dummy, it is poor form to look at either opponent's hand or at declarer's. If you do, you lose your rights as dummy. Do not stand behind declarer to see how you would play. In tournament bridge, do not discuss the previous hand with your partner if another hand is still to be played.

After the play of a hand is over, do not take an opponent's cards and look at them without asking permission. As a kibitzer (onlooker) try to watch only one hand and above all, make no facial expressions during a hand. Do not comment or talk during or between hands. If the players want the benefit of your views, they will ask for them.

Conversation at the table in serious games is generally unwelcome. Post-mortems after each hand, if limited, can be useful as long as they seek to be constructive. It is best to keep all post-mortems until the session is over and you can go over the score-sheets with your partner at leisure. During the session, conserve your energies to do battle in the next hand. It is extremely poor taste to abuse or criticise partner or an opponent. Experienced players should go out of their way to make novice players feel at ease, so that they see bridge as a pleasant recreation, not a battleground. Never try to teach anyone at the table.

Never let a harsh word pass your lips and you will be a sought-after rather than a shunned partner. Prefer to say too little than too much. If partner has bid or played the hand like an idiot, say 'bad luck' and leave it at that. Do not harp on past errors.

Use only the proper language of bridge. The correct expression when not making a bid is 'No bid' or 'Pass'. Use one and stick to the same one. Do not switch back and forth between 'Pass' and 'No bid'. Do not say 'Content', 'Okay', 'By me'. Do not say 'I'll double one heart'. Just say 'Double'. Do not say 'Spade' when you mean 'One Spade'.

Never vary the intonation in your bidding (softly on weak hands, loudly on good ones). Never put a question mark at the end of your bid to make sure that partner understands that your 4NT is Blackwood or that your double is for takeout. That would be quite atrocious. You are required to convey messages to partner by what you bid, not by the way you bid it. Frowns, scowls, raised eyebrows, etc., are out. You are not to adopt the tongue-in-cheek remark made by the legendary Groucho Marx: 'Don't bother to signal. If you like my leads, just smile. I'll understand.'

If your partner has a liberal sense of humour, you may be able to make clever remarks such as : 'When did you learn? I know this afternoon, but what time?', or in reply to 'How should I have played that hand?', 'Under an assumed name', or in reply to 'How did I play that hand?', 'Like a millionaire', or in reply to 'Did I do all right?', 'Well, you didn't knock the coffee over', but in general, bridge players are a proud lot with sensitive egos. Politeness and courtesy should be your watchword at the bridge table as in other areas of life.

Long pausing before bidding is also to be avoided, for example, the pause followed by 'Pass' tells everyone that you have 11-12 points, not quite good enough to open. Make all your bids at the same pace if you can. Sometimes you will have a serious problem which takes some time to resolve, but where this happens the obligation falls on the partner of the 'trancer' who must never take advantage of the information received from the pause.

Play your cards as a defender always at the same speed if possible. Fumbling or hesitating *with the intention of deceiving* is cheating. You must not try to mislead opponents by your manner.

In tournament bridge, if unsure about the correct procedure, always call the Tournament Director. Do not let other players tell you what the correct laws are. They are wrong more often than not. Nobody familiar with the tournament scene should mind the Director being called. It is not considered a slight, an insult, or a rebuff to the opposition.

Above all, remember that bridge is primarily a game and is meant to be enjoyed as a game. Make sure it is also enjoyable for the other players at your table. Treat your partner and the opponents like royalty and you will be a sought-after partner and not a shunned one.

APPENDIX 5 : BRIDGE MYTHS AND FALLACIES

The following common fallacies may contain a grain of truth or logic but any value vanishes when they are treated as absolute, unfailing, universal principles. At best, the following are reasonable guides which should be discarded when the circumstances warrant.

(1) Always lead top of partner's suit : No, no, a thousand times no. This approach can cost you tricks time after time. Lead top only from a doubleton or from a sequence or from three cards headed by two touching honours, but lead bottom from three or four to an honour. See Appendix 4 and pages 105-107.

(2) Always return your partner's lead : This has more merit but the rule is too wide. It is often best to return partner's lead but many situations require a switch (see Hands 31 and 32, page 106). Keep in mind the number of tricks needed to defeat the contract. Unless a passive defence is clearly indicated, avoid continuing suits which are known to be futile for beating the contract.

(3) Never lead from a king : To lead from a king-high holding is not an especially attractive lead but there are far worse combinations. It is usually more dangerous to lead away from a suit headed by the queen or by the jack and far worse in a trump contract to lead from a suit headed by the ace without the king as well. The leads of J-x or Q-x in an unbid suit are also far more dangerous than leading from a king. They become reasonable if partner has bid the suit but other than that they should be shunned. Leading from a king is acceptable when other choices are even riskier.

(4) Always cover an honour with an honour : It is only correct to cover an honour with an honour if it will promote cards in your hand or might promote winners for partner. In the trump suit in particular, it is usually wrong to cover an honour unless partner has length in trumps.

(5) Lead through strength, lead up to weakness : This has some merit but listening to the bidding and counting provide better guides for the defence. Leading through strength does not apply to the opening lead (it is rarely best to lead dummy's bid suit) and in the middle game, the rule refers to short suits (doubletons or tripletons). It is normally not in your best interests to attack dummy's or declarer's long side suit.

(6) Eight ever, nine never : When missing the queen of a long suit, good technique is to finesse for it if you have 8 cards together and to play the ace and king, hoping the queen will drop, when you have 9. When playing a complete hand, however, there can be many other considerations. Perhaps you cannot afford to lose the lead just yet and therefore cannot afford to finesse with eight trumps. Perhaps you cannot risk one particular opponent gaining the lead and so you may have to play a suit in such a way, possibly contrary to normal technique, to prevent that danger hand coming on lead.

APPENDIX 6 : COMMON CONVENTIONS & SYSTEMS

The following are brief descriptions of some conventions and systems you may come across, particularly in tournament bridge. Before adopting any of them, discuss them fully with your partner first.

1. Weak No-Trumps : Not everyone uses the same point range for the 1NT opening. The most common range for the weak 1NT is 12-14, but the 13-15 range is occasionally used, as in the Precision system.

2. Strong No-Trumps : The range for the strong no-trump is 16-18 points, but 15-17 or 15-18 point ranges are also popular. The strong no-trump is commonly used in Standard American systems.

3. Weak Twos : This refers to the approach of opening 2♡ and 2♠ (and occasionally 2◊ as well) on weak hands of 6-10 HCP with a strong 6-card suit. They are very popular in tournament bridge since they arise far more often than the strong two openings. They are both pre-emptive and constructive and the disciplined approach is not to open a weak two with a void or two singletons in the hand or with a 4-card major. Pairs using weak twos may open super-strong hands with an artificial 2♣ (see page 73).

4. Benjamin Twos : This refers to a popular treatment for two-openings in which 2♡ and 2♠ are weak twos, 2◊ is a force to game (about 23 HCP or better) and 2♣ is a strong bid but not forcing to game. 2◊ and 2♣ are both artificial openings and partner's negative reply is the next suit up. A positive reply to 2♣ is forcing to game and a positive reply to 2◊ strongly suggests slam prospects. The 2♣ opening is generally based on a strong one-suiter of around 19-22 points (8½-9½ playing tricks) or a two-suiter around the 21-22 point mark. This treatment is highly attractive because it allows a partnership to bid both weak hands and strong hands more accurately than other systems of opening two-bids.

5. Transfer Bids : A method in which a player bids the suit below the suit held, so that partner can bid the suit actually held. It is used normally only after a 1NT or 2NT opening and has many advantages over standard methods. It frequently enables the stronger hand to become declarer in suit contracts and enables a partnership to bid a greater range of hands more precisely than standard methods permit.

6. Weak Jump-Overcalls : A treatment in which a single jump-overcall is played as a weak bid, around 6-10 HCP and a 6-card or longer suit. The method is popular in tournaments but not at rubber bridge (see page 100).

7. Precision System, Big Club : Systems in which the 1♣ opening bid shows a powerful hand, usually around 16 points or more. As a consequence, opening bids other than the artificial 1♣ are limited in strength to less than the requirements for 1♣.

APPENDIX 7 : RUBBER BRIDGE

When bridge is played socially, one usually plays 'rubber bridge'. A rubber of bridge consists of two or three games ('game' being first to score 100 points or more for contracts bid and made as declarer). A rubber concludes when one side wins two games. A game is won by scoring 100 or more points when declarer.

The essential difference at rubber bridge is that part-scores are carried forward from one deal to the next. Thus, you can score the 100 points needed for game over two deals or three deals or more. It is possible to score the bonus points for game as soon as each game concludes. If so, score +350 for Game 1, +350 for Game 2 and +500 for Game 3 if games are one all and a third game is necessary. Most rubber bridge players score the game bonus points only when the rubber has ended, +700 for winning by two games to nil and +500 for winning by two games to one. It does not matter which method is used since the net result will be the same.

A rubber bridge score-sheet consists of two columns with a vertical line down the middle. It also has a horizontal line across both columns a little more than halfway down the columns. It thus looks like an inverted cross.

Trick scores are written below the horizontal line, bonus scores go above it. Your scores go in the left-hand column, theirs in the right-hand column. At the end of a game, a line is ruled across both columns below the tricks score and both sides start the next game from zero again.

At the end of a rubber, both columns are totalled. The side scoring more points is the winner. The difference between the two scores is rounded to the nearest 100 (a difference ending in 50 is rounded down). The score is then entered as the number of 100s won or lost. For example, if you won by 670, your score-sheet reads '+7' while their score-sheet would record '—7'.

There is no bonus at rubber bridge for bidding and making a part-score. Another difference at rubber bridge is that you can score bonus points simply for being lucky enough to have good cards, for holding 'honours'. As you know, the honour cards are the A, K, Q, J and 10. Score 150 points for all 5 trump honours in one hand, 100 points for any 4 of the 5 trump honours in one hand, or 150 points for 4 aces in one hand, but only if the contract is no-trumps.

Bonuses for honours are scored whether or not the contract is made. Honours may be held by declarer, dummy or either defender. In order not to tell the opposition what cards you hold, honours are usually claimed after the hand has been played. Honours are not scored when playing Chicago or duplicate.

Other scoring is essentially the same as for Chicago or duplicate and a full rubber bridge scoring table is on the next page.

RUBBER BRIDGE SCORING TABLE

POINTS TOWARDS GAME UNDER THE LINE :

No-trumps —	First trick	40
	Subsequent tricks	30
Spades or Hearts (major suits) Each trick		30
Diamonds or Clubs (minor suits) Each trick		20

Final contract doubled and made : Double the above values
Final contract redoubled and made : Above values x 4

BONUS POINTS ABOVE THE LINE :

OVERTRICKS

		Not vulnerable	*Vulnerable*
For each	Not doubled	Trick value	Trick value
overtrick	Doubled	100	200
	Redoubled	200	400

SLAMS BID AND MADE

	Not vulnerable	*Vulnerable*
Small slam	500	750
Grand slam	1000	1500

FOR DEFEATING A CONTRACT :

Not doubled, each undertrick : 50 not vulnerable, 100 if vulnerable
Doubled, not vulnerable : 1st undertrick 100, 2nd and 3rd 200, others 300
Doubled and vulnerable : 1st undertrick 200, all others 300
Redoubled : All undertricks score at twice the doubled rate above

FOR MAKING A DOUBLED CONTRACT :   50

FOR MAKING A REDOUBLED CONTRACT :   100

FOR HONOURS :

Four trump honours in one hand	100
Five trump honours in one hand	150
Four aces in one hand if the contract is no-trumps	150

(Either side can score honours which are claimed at the end of play.)

FOR WINNING THE RUBBER :

For winning by two games to nil	700
For winning by two games to one	500
For one game if the rubber is unfinished	300
For part-score if rubber is unfinished	50

(If scoring game by game : Game 1 : 350,   Game 2 : 350,   Game 3 : 500.)

APPENDIX 8 : TOURNAMENT BRIDGE

The main kinds of competitive bridge are pairs events and teams events. Bridge is played internationally. In each odd-numbered year there are the Bermuda Bowl (World Open Teams) and the Venice Cup (World Women's Teams) in which 16 teams representing different geographical zones compete. Every four years in the 'Bridge Olympiad' a far greater number of teams compete. In recent years, more than sixty countries have been represented at these Olympiads. In the other even-numbered years there are the World Pairs Championships (open pairs, womens pairs, mixed pairs) as well as the Rosenblum Cup (another World Open Teams).

Each country conducts national championships and many tournaments of lower status. There are also tournaments to select the players who will represent their country.

Many clubs conduct an Individual Championship once a year. In pairs and teams events, you keep the same partner for each session and usually throughout the event. In an Individual each competitor plays with every other competitor for one, two or three deals. Individuals are not considered serious events since partnership understanding tends to be minimal. A calm temperament is a prerequisite to surviving an Individual.

In general, pairs events are more common than any other type of event. The advantage of tournament bridge is that the element of having good cards or bad cards is reduced to a minimum, since all players play exactly the same deals. Another advantage is that you can compete against the top players merely by playing in the same tournament. In few other sports could a novice play against a world champion in a tournament. Tournament bridge also improves your game, since hand records are available to check afterwards where you may have gone wrong.

There are some differences between tournament bridge and rubber bridge in regard to technicalities and strategy. Except at the first table, you will not shuffle and deal the cards. The cards come to you in a tray, called a 'board' and you must put the cards back in the correct slot after the board has been played. The board is marked N, E, S and W, and must be placed properly on the table. The board also states which side is vulnerable and who is the dealer. During the play, the cards are not thrown into the middle of the table. Each player keeps the cards in front of them, turning the cards face down after the trick is over. You may examine the trick just played only while your card remains face up. Tricks won are placed in front of you and perpendicular to the table. Tricks lost are placed parallel to the edge of the table in front of you. After the hand is over, you still have your original thirteen cards and can see at a glance how many tricks have been won and how many lost.

Each board in tournament bridge is scored independently. In rubber bridge if you make a part-score you have an advantage for the next deal, but in tournament bridge you do not carry forward any scores. You enter the score for the hand played, and on the next board both sides start from zero again.

As each deal is totally unrelated to what happened on the previous deal, there are significant scoring differences in tournament bridge :

(1) Honours do not count (unless otherwise stated by the tournament rules).

(2) For bidding and making a part-score, add 50 to the trick total.

(3) For bidding and making a game not vulnerable, add 300 to the trick total.

(4) For bidding and making a game vulnerable, add 500 to the trick total.

The result you obtain on the board is entered on the 'travelling score-sheet' at the back of the board. You may not look at that until the hand is over, since it contains a record of the hand and also how other pairs fared on the board. Your score on each board is compared with the scores of every other pair that played the board. If you are North-South, your real opponents are all the other North-South pairs, not the particular East-West pair you play each time. On each board, a certain number of match-points is awarded (usually two less than the number of pairs who play the board). If 15 pairs play a board, the best score receives 28 match-points, a 'top', the next best score receives 26 and so on down to the worst score which receives 0, a 'bottom'. An average score would receive 14 match-points. You are awarded 2 points for each pair your score beats and 1 point for each pair with whom your score ties.

The scoring is done once for the North-South pairs and then for the East-West pairs. Obviously, if a North-South pair scores a top, the corresponding East-West pair against whom they played the board gets a bottom. Each pair's points over all the boards are totalled and the pair with the highest number of match-points wins.

Tactics in pairs events differ from those in rubber bridge. Careful declarer play and defence are the order of the day. Every overtrick and every undertrick could be vital. They make the difference between good scores and bad scores. In rubber bridge, declarer's aim is almost always to make the contract and the defence's aim is to defeat it. At pairs the aim is to obtain the best possible score which may mean from declarer's viewpoint that making the contract is a secondary consideration while from the defenders' viewpoint, the possibility of giving away an overtrick in trying to defeat the contract may be unwarranted.

Being extremely competitive in the bidding is essential. Almost always force the opposition to the three-level on part-score deals. Be quick to re-open the bidding if they stop at a very low level in a suit. In pairs events, re-opening the bidding occurs ten times more often than at rubber bridge.

Minor suit contracts at the game zone, should be avoided. Prefer 3NT to 5♣ or 5♦, even if 3NT is riskier, since making an overtrick in 3NT scores more than a minor suit game. On the other hand, it is not necessary to bid borderline games or close slams. The reward for success is not so great in pairs events as to justify 24 point games or 31 point slams. You should be in game or in slam if it has a 50% or better chance. If less, you will score better by staying out of it.

What counts at duplicate pairs is how often a certain strategy will work for you, not the size of the result. If a certain action scores 50 extra points 8 times out of 10, but loses 500 twice, it is sensible at duplicate but ridiculous at rubber bridge. Penalty doubles are far more frequent at pairs since players are anxious to improve their score. The rule about a two-trick safety margin is frequently disregarded since one down, doubled, vulnerable, may be a top-score while one down, undoubled, vulnerable, may be below average.

Safety plays which involve sacrificing a trick to ensure the contract almost never apply in pairs, unless the contract you have reached is an unbelievably good one.

In the tournament world you will encounter a remarkable number and variety of systems and conventions and gradually you will come to recognise them. The more important ones have been listed in Appendix 6. A most important point to remember is that a bidding system is not some secret between you and your partner. You and your partner are not allowed to have any secret understanding about your bids. That is *cheating*. A bidding system is not a secret code. The opponents are entitled to know as much about what the bidding means as you or your partner. If they ask you what you understand by a certain bid of your partner's, you must tell them truthfully. Of course, partner's bid may be meaningless and if you cannot understand it, all you can do is to be honest and tell the opposition that you do not know what partner's bid means.

Similarly, if you do not understand the opposition's bidding, you are entitled to ask. When it is your turn to bid but before you make your bid, you ask the partner of the bidder 'Could you please explain the auction?' You may ask during the auction or after the auction has ended, when it is your turn to play. Unless it affects your making a bid, prefer to wait until the auction is over. After all, the opposition might not understand their bidding either and when you ask, they may well realise their mistake.

If an irregularity occurs at the table, do not be dismayed if the Director is called. That is a normal part of the game and it is the Director's job to keep the tournament running smoothly and to sort out any irregularities.

ANSWERS TO EXERCISES AND BIDDING PRACTICE

Page Answers

27 **Exercise 1 :** 1. Unbalanced   2. Unbalanced   3. Semi-balanced
4. Balanced 5. Balanced 6. Balanced 7. Unbalanced 8. Unbalanced

Exercise 2 :	A	B	C	D
Hand 1	13	Semi-balanced	2-5-4-2	2-suiter
Hand 2	14	Balanced	4-4-2-3	2-suiter
Hand 3	14	Balanced	3-4-3-3	1-suiter
Hand 4	13	Unbalanced	5-5-1-2	2-suiter
Hand 5	11	Semi-balanced	2-3-6-2	1-suiter
Hand 6	12	Unbalanced	5-0-2-6	2-suiter
Hand 7	14	Unbalanced	4-1-4-4	3-suiter
Hand 8	13	Unbalanced	6-0-3-4	2-suiter

34 **A.** 1. One no-trump 2. One club 3. One spade 4. One club
5. One no-trump 6. One spade   7. One heart   8. One no-trump

B. 1. Pass   2. 3NT   3. 2NT   4. 3NT

Partnership Bidding Practice :

	W	E		W	E		W	E		W	E
1.	No	1NT	2.	1NT	2NT	3.	No	1NT	4.	1NT	2NT
	No			No			2NT	3NT		No	
							No				

	W	E		W	E		W	E		W	E
5.	No	1NT	6.	1NT	3NT	7.	1♣	1♠	8.	1♣	1◇
	2NT	3NT		No			1NT	3NT		3NT	No
	No						No				

39 1. One heart. Middle suit with a 4-4-4-1 and a black singleton.
2. One diamond   3. One diamond. Bid the suit below the singleton
with a 4-4-4-1 when you have a red singleton.   4. One club
5. One club   6. One spade. Longest suit comes first. 7. One spade
8. One heart   9. No bid   10. One diamond. Start with the higher
suit with a 5-5 pattern.   11. One club. The cheaper suit comes first
with a 4-4-3-2 pattern.   12. One spade   13. 2NT (20-22 points)
14. One diamond   15. One club   16. 1NT (12-14) 17. No bid
18. 2NT   19. Two clubs (23 HCP or more)   20. 1NT
21. One club   22. One heart   23. One spade   24. One diamond

46 **A.** 1. One spade 2. One diamond   3. Two clubs. You have club
support and no other suit to show.   4. One heart. Bid the cheaper
4-card suit. 5. One diamond   6. One spade. Prefer a new suit to
raising a minor.   7. One spade. Bid the higher suit first with a 5-5
pattern.   8. One heart. Show a major rather support the minor.
Support the minor next round if partner does not raise the major.

46 **B.**   1. One spade. Up-the-line : 1♠ is cheaper than 2♣.
2. One spade   3. 1NT. Not enough for 2♣, showing 10+ points
4. 1NT. The 1NT response does not promise a balanced hand.
5. Two hearts   6. Two hearts. With 6-9 points, prefer raising a
major suit to a change of suit.   7. Two hearts   8. Two hearts

C. (a) 1. One diamond 2. One diamond (up-the-line) 3. One spade
4. One heart 5. One heart 6. One diamond 7. One heart
8. One diamond. Do not raise a minor and bypass a major suit.

(b) 1. One spade. Majors first. 2. One spade 3. One spade
4. One heart. There is no suit quality test for a response.
5. One heart 6. One spade 7. One heart. Not strong enough for
two clubs which would show 10+ total points. 8. One heart

(c) 1. One spade. Not enough for two diamonds (10+ points)
2. One spade 3. One spade 4. Two hearts 5. Two hearts
6. One spade 7. Two hearts 8. Two hearts

(d) 1. Two spades 2. Two spades 3. Two spades 4. Two spades
5. Two spades 6. Four spades. The shape is exceptional.
7. 1NT. No strong enough for two clubs. 8. 1NT

54

	W	E		W	E		W	E		W	E
9.	1♣	1◇	10.	1♣	1♠	11.	1♣	1♡	12.	1♣	2♣
	1♠	1NT		2NT	3♡		3NT	4♡		No	
	No			4♡	No		No				
13.	No	1♣	14.	No	1♣	15.	No	1♣	16.	1♠	1NT
	1♡	2NT		1◇	1♠		1♠	4♠		3♡	4♡
	3◇	4♡		1NT	2NT		No			No	
	No			No							
17.	No	1♡	18.	No	1♠	19.	No	1◇	20.	1♣	1◇
	1NT	2◇		1NT	2♡		1NT	No		1NT	2◇
	2♡	No		No						No	
21.	No	1♣	22.	1♣	1♡						
	1♡	1♠		1♠	2♠						
	2♠	No		4♠	No						

62 **A.** 1. 3NT 2. One diamond 3. One diamond. Not 3NT because
you have no spade stopper. 4. One heart 5. One diamond
6. One heart 7. One diamond 8. One heart. You have enough for
a slam but you cannot yet tell which slam is best.

62 **B.** 1. 3 diamonds 2. 1 heart 3. 1 heart 4. 1 spade
5. 2 spades, because the spades are so strong. 6. 1 spade. The
spades are not good enough for two spades. 7. 2 clubs. You are
too strong for 3 diamonds. 8. 2 clubs. Longest suit first.

C. 1. 1 spade. Bid 4 hearts next round. You are too strong for either
3 hearts or 4 hearts. 2. 1 spade 3. 2 clubs (up-the-line)
4. 2 diamonds. Higher suit first with 5-5 patterns.

D. 1. 2 diamonds 2. 2 hearts 3. 2 diamonds 4. 3 spades

62 **E.** 1. 3 spades. This shows five spades and is forcing to game.
2. 3NT. With game interest, stay with no-trumps rather than show a
minor. Counting Length Points, you are worth 14 which is enough to
bid 3NT opposite 1NT. 3. 4 hearts. You know you have at least eight
hearts together and 4 hearts should be safer than 3 no-trumps.

62 **E. 4.** 3 hearts. Forcing to game and shows five hearts. If partner bids 3NT denying heart support, you can bid 4 diamonds, intending to reach at least 6 diamonds.

65 **A.** 1. 3NT   2. 3NT. Your hand is balanced and you have more than enough to raise to 3NT.   3. 3 clubs   4. 3NT. You can risk 3NT with a semi-balanced hand as partner has promised a heart stopper.

B. 1. 2NT   2. 3NT   3. 2 diamonds. You are not strong enough for 2 hearts. Bidding at the two-level above the suit opened shows at least 16 points.   4. 2 hearts. Now you are strong enough to 'reverse'. 5. 3 clubs   6. 4 clubs   7. 3 diamonds   8. 2 hearts. You are strong enough for 3 diamonds but show a major rather than rebid a minor.

C. 1. 2 diamonds. Bidding a lower-ranking suit at the two-level does not show any extra values.   2. 2 hearts. Not enough for 2 spades. 3. 2 hearts   4. 3 clubs. Raising partner does not promise extra. 5. 2NT   6. 2 spades   7. 3 hearts   8. 3 diamonds. Shows a strong hand (16+ points, forcing to game) and at least a 5-5 pattern.

D. 1. 3 clubs. Shows 5 hearts-4 clubs at least.   2. 4 hearts. You know you have at least eight hearts together.   3. No bid.   4. 3 diamonds. Suggest a suit contract if your hand is unbalanced.

E. 1. 2 hearts. Show a second suit rather than repeat your first suit. 2. 2 spades. However, if you bid beyond two of the suit opened, you are showing 16 points or more. Here you are not strong enough for 3 clubs. 3. 3 spades. Shows 6+ spades and 16+ points, forcing to game. 4. 4 spades. Your spades are strong enough to insist on having spades as trumps. Count the number of cards in your long suit (seven) and the honours in that suit. If the total is 10 or more, your suit is self-sufficient and you can insist on your suit as trumps.

66

	W	E		W	E		W	E		W	E
23.	1♣	1♦	24.	1♣	1♦	25.	1♣	1♥	26.	1♣	1♥
	1♠	3NT		1♠	3NT		3♣	3♦		2♣	2♦
	No			4♠	5♣		3NT	No		2♥	4♥
				No						No	
27.	1♣	1♦	28.	1♣	1♦	29.	1♣	1♦	30.	1♥	2NT
	1♥	4♥		1♥	3♦		3♦	3NT		4♥	No
	No			3NT	No		No				
31.	1♦	1♥	32.	1♦	2♣	33.	1♦	1♥	34.	1♦	1♥
	2♣	3♣		2♦	2♥		2♣	3♥		2♦	3NT
	3NT	No		4♥	No		4♥	No		No	
35.	1♦	1♥	36.	1♦	1♥						
	2♣	3NT		1♠	3♠						
	No			4♠	No						

67

	W	E		W	E		W	E		W	E
37.	1♥	1♠	38.	1♥	1♠	39.	1♥	2♣	40.	1♥	2♣
	2♠	4♠		2♥	3♣		2♦	2NT		2♠	3♣
	No			3NT	No		3NT	No		3NT	No

67 | 41. 1♥ 1♠ | 42. 1♥ 2♦ | 43. 1♥ 2♦ | 44. 1♠ 2♦
3♠ 4♠ | 3♦ No | 3♦ 4♥ | 2♥ 4♠
No | | No | No

45. 1♠ 2♦ | 46. 1♠ 2♦ | 47. 1♠ 2♥ | 48. 1♠ 2♥
2♥ 4♥ | 2♥ 2NT | 3♦ 3♥ | 2♠ No
No | 3NT No | 4♥ No

49. 1♠ 2♥ | 50. 1♠ 2♦
3♥ 4♥ | 2♥ 3♥
No | 4♥ No

72   **A.** 1. 2NT   2. 1 heart   3. 2 spades (strong suit)   4. 3 clubs

B. 1. 3 hearts   2. 2 hearts   3. 2NT   4. 2 spades (strong suit)
5. 1 spade   6. 2 diamonds   7. 1NT   8. 3 hearts

51.	W	E	52.	W	E	53.	W	E
	No	1♥		No	1♣		No	1♠
	3♥	4♥		1♥	1♠		2♦	No
	No			3♠	4♠			
				No				

54.	W	E	55.	W	E	56.	W	E
	No	1♣		No	1♥		No	1♠
	1♠	No		2♣	2NT		2♣	No
				3NT	No			

75   **A.** 1. 2 hearts   2. 2 clubs (artificial)   3. 2 spades   4. 1 spade
5. 2 hearts. Follow up with 6 diamonds.   This sequence describes the
freak nature of your hand.   6. 2 clubs

B. 1. 2 diamonds (artificial negative, 0-7 points)   2. 2 diamonds
3. 2NT   4. 3 diamonds   5. 2 hearts   6. 2 hearts   7. 3 diamonds
8. 2NT

C. 1. 2NT   2. 2NT   3. 3NT   4. 3 diamonds   5. 3 hearts
6. 3 hearts   7. 3 diamonds   8. 3 hearts

D. 1. 2 spades   2. 4 spades   3. 2 spades   4. 2NT   5. 3NT
6. 2NT   7. 3 diamonds   8. 3 clubs   9. 3 clubs

76   **E.** 1. 3 spades   2. 3 spades   3. 4 spades   4. 4 diamonds
5. 4 hearts (3 hearts is forcing.)   6. 3 spades   7. 3NT 8. 4 hearts

F. 1. 6 hearts   2. No bid   3. 7 diamonds   4. 7 hearts

76

	W	E		W	E		W	E		W	E
57.	2♣	2♦	58.	No	2♣	59.	2♠	2NT	60.	No	2♣
	3♦	3♥		2♦	3♣		3♠	No		2♦	2NT
	3♠	3NT		3NT	4♠		4♠			3NT	No
	No			No							

	W	E		W	E		W	E		W	E
61.	2♦	2NT	62.	No	2♣	63.	No	2♣	64.	2♣	2♦
	3♦	3♠		2♦	2♠		2♦	2NT		2♠	2NT
	3NT	No		3♣	3♥		3♥	4♥		6♣	7♠
				4♥	No		No			No	

83   **A.**   1. Slam zone   2. Slam zone   3. Game zone   4. Game zone
5. Game zone   6. Slam zone

B.   1. 5 spades   2. 5 clubs (shows 0 or 4 aces)   3. 4 clubs. As the diamonds are unguarded, cue-bidding is better than Blackwood.
4. 5 diamonds   5. 5 hearts. North's 5 clubs = cue bid. Your 5 hearts = ace of hearts and denies ace of diamonds   6. 6 diamonds (1 king)

84   **C. a.** 6 spades. With one ace missing, bid the small slam. Do not stop in 5 spades.   **b.** 6 spades. One king is missing and you cannot tell which one it is.   **c.** 7NT. Partner has shown spade support plus 3 aces and 2 kings. That gives you thirteen tricks easily.

D. a. 4 diamonds, a cue bid showing first round control in diamonds.
b. 4 spades. With no ace or void to show, return to the trump suit.
c. 5 clubs. 4 clubs, 4 diamonds and 4 hearts = cue bids showing first round control in the suits bid. 5 clubs, a suit that has been cue-bid previously, shows second round control in clubs.
d. 5 hearts. 4 clubs and 4 hearts = first round controls. 5 clubs = second round club control. 4 hearts denied first round control in diamonds and now 5 hearts denies second round control in diamonds.

84   **65.**

W	E
2♣	3♣
3♠	4♦
4NT	5♣
6NT	No

66.

W	E
1NT	6NT
No	

67.

W	E
No	2♣
2NT	3♥
4♥	4NT
5♦	5NT
6♦	7NT
No	

68.

W	E
1♠	2♣
2♥	4♥
4NT	5♥
5NT	6♦
6♥	No

69.

W	E
1♦	1♥
3♣	4♣
4♦	4♥
5♣	No

(4♦ = cue, 4♥ = cue)

70.

W	E
2♣	2♦
2♥	3♥
4NT	5♣
5NT	6♥
7NT	No

90   **A.**   1. 8   2. 7   3. 6   4. 7   5. 6   6. 6   7. 7   8. 4
9. 6   10. 7   11. 6   12. 5   13. 5   14. 4   15. 6

90   **B. (i)**   1. 4 spades   2. 4 hearts   3. 1 club   4. 3NT   5. 4 spades
6. 3 clubs (3NT needs seven winners)   7. No bid
8. No bid. Do not pre-empt with a 4-card major suit as well.
9. No bid   10. No bid. Your suit is too weak
11. 1 heart   12. 4 hearts

(ii)   1. 3 spades   2. 3 hearts   3. 1 club   4. 3NT   5. 4 spades
6. No bid   7. No bid   8. No bid   9. No bid   10. No bid
11. 1 heart   12. 3 hearts

91   **C. (i)**   1. No bid   2. No bid   3. No bid. Do not rescue a pre-empt with a weak hand.   4. 3 spades. New suit is forcing.   5. No bid 6. 4 hearts   7. 3NT. You have a double stopper in each outside suit. 8. 4 hearts   9. 4 hearts   10. No bid   11. 4NT, asking for aces. If partner has the ace of hearts, you can count 13 tricks. 12. 4NT. If partner has one ace, you have enough for 6 hearts.

(ii) 1. No bid   2. No bid   3. No bid. Opposite a vulnerable pre-empt, you need more than two winners to justify a bid.   4. 3 spades 5. 4 hearts. You have three possible winners for partner. 6. 4 hearts 7. 3NT   8. 4 hearts   9. 4 hearts   10. No bid   11. 4NT   12. 4NT

71.	W	E	72.	W	E	73.	W	E
	3♠	4♠		3◊	3NT		3◊	3♠
	No			No			4♠	No

74.	W	E	75.	W	E	76.	W	E
	No	3♡		4♠	4NT		3◊	3♡
	No			5◊	6♠		4♡	4NT
				No			5◊	6♡
							No	

101   **A.** 1. No bid   2. 1NT   3. 2 clubs   4. No bid. With length and strength in the enemy suit, the best strategy in most cases is to pass and defend.

B.   1. 1 spade   2. 1 spade   3. No bid   4. 1 diamond   5. No bid 6. 4 spades   7. 1 spade. With a 5-5 pattern, start with the higher-ranking suit. 8. 2 hearts. Strong jump overcall. 9. No bid

C. 1. 2 diamonds 2. No bid. Suit too weak to overcall. 3. 3 clubs. Strong jump overcall. You hope partner can bid 3NT.   4. 3NT. You figure to take nine tricks on a spade lead. 3NT is a good gamble. 5. 2 hearts   6. No bid   7. 5 diamonds. Pre-emptive. Worth the risk. 8. 2 diamonds   9. No bid. The clubs do not meet the Suit Quality Test for 2 clubs and the spade length is a drawback to an overcall.

102   **D.** 1. No bid   2. 1 spade   3. 4 spades. Bid up on the freak hands.

E. 1. No bid. If the opponents' bidding is genuine, partner can have scarcely one point. 2. 4 hearts. A reasonable shot. 3. Pass. As with the first hand, partner can have very little. Your hand is good for defending, not for playing with only 5-6 tricks potential.

102   **F.** 1. No bid   2. 4 hearts   3. 2 hearts   4. 3 hearts 5. 2 diamonds   6. 1NT   7. 2NT   8. 1 spade   9. 3NT

G. 1. 3 spades   2. 4 spades   3. 3 spades (2NT is also possible, as you have their suit well stopped)   4. 4 spades (3NT is possible) 5. 3 diamonds   6. 4 spades

103 **Partnership Bidding :** 77. (1 club) : 1 heart : INT, 2 hearts : No bid
78. (1 club) : 1 no-trump : 4 hearts, No bid
79. (1 diamond) : 2 hearts : 4 hearts, No bid
80. (1 diamond) : 1 heart : 3 hearts, 4 hearts : No bid
81. (1 heart) : 1NT : 2NT, 3NT : No bid
82. (1 heart) : 2 spades : 4 spades, No bid
83. (1 heart) : 2 diamonds : 2 spades, 3 spades : 4 spades, No bid
84. (1 spade) : 2 clubs : 2NT, 3NT : No bid
85. (1 spade) : 3 hearts : 4 hearts, No bid
86. (1 spade) : 2 clubs : 3NT, No bid

110 **A.** 1. Takeout   2. Takeout   3. Takeout   4. Penalties
5. Penalties. Double of a 1NT opening is for penalties.
6. Penalties. Double after partner has bid is for penalties.

B. 1. Double   2. Double   3. 1 diamond. Lack of support for
hearts makes double unattractive.   4. Double. If partner bids
diamonds, you can bid hearts.   5. Double. The hand is too powerful
for even a strong jump-overcall.   6. 1 spade. With a 5-5, bid the
higher suit first. Lack of heart support makes a double unappealing.
7. Double.   8. 1NT. If the hand fits a 1NT overcall, prefer that bid.
9. Double. Double-and-NT-later is stronger than 1NT at once.

C. 1. No bid 2. No bid 3. Double   4. 1 spade. Prefer to show a
strong 5-card or longer holding in the other major by bidding the major.
5. Double   6. No bid   7. 1NT   8. Double. Too strong for 1NT.
9. Double. Then bid the spades later.

111 **D.** 1. 1 spade   2. 1 spade. This hand makes Hand 1 look great.
3. 1 spade 4. 1 heart. Choose a major rather than a minor in reply
to a double even when the major is shorter or weaker.   5. 2 clubs
6. 1 heart. With no 4-card suit to bid (you would not want to bid
their suit), choose your cheapest 3-card suit.

E. 1. 2 spades. Too strong for 1 spade. Worth 10 points counting 3
for your singleton. 2. 2 hearts. Too big for 1 heart. Count your
doubletons and you have 10 points. 3. 2 diamonds. Not 1 diamond.
4. 1NT   5. 2NT   6. 4 spades. A sound approach when
answering a takeout double is to imagine partner has opened in
your best suit. If partner had opened 1 spade, you would not settle
for less than game.

111 **F.** 1. No bid. You are no longer obliged to bid.   2. 2 hearts.
However, you are not forced to pass. Over an intervening bid, you
should bid with 6 points or more. Again, imagine partner had
opened 1 heart. You would not hesitate then to bid 2 hearts over a
1 spade overcall.   3. 3 hearts. If you are worth a jump, make the
jump reply over the intervention (but not beyond game, of course).
Had South passed, you would have jumped to 2 hearts.

G. 1. No bid   2. 2 hearts 3. 3 hearts. Partner may have 0 points.

112   87. (1 heart) : Double : 2 diamonds, No bid
      88. (1 heart) : Double : 2 clubs, No bid
      89. (1 club) : Double: 1 spade, 2 spades : No bid
      90. (1 club) : Double : 1 heart, 3 hearts : No bid
      91. (1 diamond) : Double : 1 spade, No bid
      92. (1 heart) : Double : 1NT, 2NT : 3NT, No bid
      93. (1 spade): Double : 2NT, 3NT : No bid
      94. (1 heart) : Double : 2 spades, No bid
      95. (1 club) : Double : 4 spades, No bid
      96. (1 diamond) : Double : 3 clubs, 3 hearts : 4 hearts, No bid

135   **1.** a. 2, second hand low   b. Ace. Capture their honour.
c. 3. When an honour card is led from dummy, do not cover if
dummy also holds the card below it. Cover only when the last card
of the cards in sequence is led.   d. 3, second hand low. Perhaps
South holds the K-J and may misguess the finesse if you play low.

2. a. Ace. Grab the lead and cash your club winners which will
defeat the 3NT contract.   b. 4, second hand low   c. 4. Since
dummy has only ace doubleton, do not cover the queen with the
king. Your king will come good by the third round of the suit.
d. Play low. Playing the queen cannot create any tricks for partner.

3. a. K. Cheapest of equally high cards. b. K   c. Q   d. 9   e. 8

4. a. K.   b. J   c. J   d. 9. As good as the 10 or J.   e. 10

136   **5.** a. 9. High card signal = encouraging.   b. 2. Lowest card = no
interest in the suit you are leading.   c. A. Overtake with the ace
and return the 3 to partner's known queen and ruff the third round.
d. Overtake the king with the ace, cash the queen and let partner
ruff the third round. Partner's king lead when you hold the queen
must be a singleton or a doubleton. If it is a singleton, partner will
be unable to play a second round.   e. 5. Start of an encouraging
high-low signal. The 5 is not high but it is the highest you can afford.

6. Discard the 2 of hearts or the 2 of spades. You want a club
switch but you cannot afford to signal with the 10 or jack of clubs.

7. (a) South has the queen. Partner would play third hand high.
(b) South has the 8. Partner's 9, third hand high, denies the 8.
(c) East has the 10. Otherwise South would have won with the 10.
Therefore, East began with 10-9 doubleton and South with A-Q-8.

8. (a) South has the king. With K-J, East would play the K, third
hand high. (b) South has the 9. With J-9 over dummy's 10, East
would play the 9.   (c) East has the 7. Since South can be placed
with A-K-9 in hearts, South cannot have the 7 as well because
South denied a 4-card major in reply to the Stayman enquiry.

9. (a) 8, top from a remaining doubleton.   (b) 2, the original
fourth-highest.   (c) 4, the original fourth-highest. (d) Q, top of
the remaining doubleton. (e) J, top of touching honours.

Play Hands for NORTH (* = dealer)

1*	2	3	4	5*	6
♠AKJ7	♠KQ109	♠7543	♠J92	♠AJ72	♠K105
♥943	♥32	♥QJ109	♥AK2	♥Q53	♥875
♦875	♦J6	♦KQ10	♦KQJ	♦942	♦QJ862
♣642	♣98754	♣106	♣8632	♣J62	♣74

7	8	9*	10	11	12
♠AK	♠KJ1082	♠AKQ983	♠106	♠53	♠54
♥1062	♥987	♥A86	♥82	♥92	♥86
♦QJ109	♦Q9	♦Q3	♦9843	♦KQ93	♦A1093
♣AQ72	♣Q108	♣J10	♣K10642	♣J8742	♣107542

13*	14	15	16	17*	18
♠1074	♠---	♠A975	♠---	♠AQJ3	♠Q109
♥AKQ10	♥J1054	♥KQ42	♥109632	♥AK	♥J10953
♦K	♦A753	♦852	♦97542	♦A1042	♦98
♣J8762	♣87432	♣KQ	♣AK8	♣QJ9	♣A87

19	20	21*	22	23	24
♠K	♠9	♠9652	♠86	♠AKQJ2	♠Q109
♥86532	♥QJ974	♥J10943	♥K7532	♥KQJ4	♥J1098
♦7432	♦KJ1074	♦652	♦A2	♦AQJ	♦Q109
♣753	♣92	♣8	♣AKJ5	♣2	♣965

25*	26	27	28	29*	30
♠AKQ9765	♠KQ76	♠J	♠106432	♠AK	♠65
♥2	♥K10873	♥AQJ	♥---	♥K862	♥2
♦8	♦J98	♦K109	♦K932	♦KQ1093	♦J7643
♣9873	♣2	♣A98763	♣10876	♣105	♣J7542

31	32	33*	34	35	36
♠52	♠AK	♠J108743	♠8	♠AKQJ	♠KQJ107
♥A932	♥A109852	♥6	♥KJ10654	♥A753	♥K862
♦82	♦K3	♦1095	♦A6	♦K	♦94
♣J9864	♣KJ10	♣J53	♣J962	♣Q1098	♣A10

1	2*	3	4	5	6*
♠942	♠AJ3	♠AK102	♠108753	♠965	♠A32
♥852	♥Q54	♥A4	♥Q76	♥J10942	♥J1042
♦QJ10	♦AK52	♦643	♦972	♦85	♦K95
♣KQ105	♣1063	♣8532	♣K9	♣K105	♣1063

7	8	9	10*	11	12
♠QJ52	♠A75	♠J	♠AQ43	♠7642	♠732
♥54	♥A6	♥KQJ1053	♥AK7	♥107	♥QJ1095
♦A43	♦KJ43	♦AJ82	♦KQ1072	♦AJ108	♦KJ72
♣J985	♣AK95	♣93	♣9	♣A109	♣6

13	14*	15	16	17	18*
♠952	♠976432	♠108632	♠K52	♠754	♠J8643
♥- - -	♥AKQ	♥J865	♥QJ7	♥9542	♥87
♦1087654	♦KJ	♦94	♦KQJ	♦KQJ9	♦5432
♣10543	♣Q9	♣75	♣J942	♣103	♣53

19	20	21	22*	23	24
♠9742	♠AKQ8432	♠AK7	♠KQ10	♠96543	♠AJ73
♥K107	♥A6	♥A82	♥QJ8	♥A8	♥KQ
♦965	♦A2	♦AQ3	♦84	♦K2	♦873
♣AKQ	♣J8	♣QJ54	♣Q9762	♣9654	♣QJ104

25	26*	27	28	29	30*
♠10	♠42	♠AQ1097	♠A95	♠6543	♠Q842
♥KQJ83	♥Q4	♥K5432	♥K854	♥95	♥QJ107
♦AJ5	♦63	♦7	♦A6	♦A	♦Q98
♣6542	♣KQJ8763	♣102	♣AKQ	♣AQJ863	♣K9

31	32	33	34*	35	36
♠AKJ984	♠Q6	♠A2	♠J543	♠109742	♠5
♥K	♥J	♥98732	♥AQ2	♥1086	♥AQJ10
♦K75	♦QJ10964	♦K3	♦KQJ84	♦1093	♦AQ52
♣1053	♣AQ87	♣Q1062	♣Q	♣J4	♣K872

Play Hands for SOUTH (* = dealer)

1	2	3*	4	5	6
♠Q 3	♠5 4 2	♠9 8 6	♠K Q	♠K Q 8	♠Q J 9 4
♡A 7 6	♡A J 10 9 8 7	♡K 8 7 5	♡J 4 3	♡K 7 6	♡A 9 6
◇A 4 3 2	◇Q 10 8 7	◇A 9 7	◇A 10 6 5 3	◇A 6 3	◇10 7
♣A 9 7 3	♣- - -	♣9 7 4	♣Q J 4	♣A 9 8 3	♣J 9 8 5

7*	8	9	10	11*	12
♠9 8 6 3	♠Q 3	♠7 6 5 4	♠7 5 2	♠A K 9	♠K Q J 10 6
♡A K 8 3	♡K 5 4 3	♡9 7 2	♡Q J 10 9 3	♡A K 8 6 4 3	♡A 7 3
◇8 6 2	◇10 8 7 6 5	◇9 5 4	◇A 6	◇7 6	◇5 4
♣K 3	♣J 4	♣A K Q	♣A Q 8	♣Q 5	♣J 9 8

13	14	15*	16	17*	18
♠Q J	♠Q 10 8	♠K	♠Q 9 8 6	♠8 6 2	♠- - -
♡7 6 5 4 3	♡9 6	♡A 10 7 3	♡A 5	♡Q J 8 7 6 3	♡A 6 4 2
◇Q J 3 2	◇10 8 6 2	◇J 6 3	◇8 6 3	◇7	◇Q 10 7
♣A K	♣A K 10 5	♣A J 10 9 3	♣Q 10 7 5	♣8 6 5	♣J 10 9 6 4 2

19*	20	21	22	23*	24
♠A Q 8 6	♠J 10 5	♠10 8 3	♠A 2	♠7	♠- - -
♡A Q J	♡10 3	♡7 5	♡A 9 6 4	♡10 9 7 5 3 2	♡7 6 5 4 3 2
◇A K Q	◇Q 5	◇J 10 9 8	◇K Q J 7 6	◇6 3	◇J 6 2
♣J 4 2	♣A K 6 5 4 3	♣A 10 7 6	♣8 3	♣A K J 3	♣A 7 3 2

25	26	27*	28	29	30
♠4 2	♠J 8 5	♠8	♠K Q J 8	♠Q J 7 2	♠A 7
♡A 7	♡J 9 2	♡10 7	♡Q 9	♡A Q J 10 7	♡A 8 6 5 4 3
◇9 7 6 4 3 2	◇Q 7 5 4 2	◇A Q J 8 6 5 4 3 2	◇8 7 5 4	◇J 4	◇A K
♣Q J 10	♣A 10	♣5	♣9 5 2	♣9 4	♣10 6 3

31*	32	33	34	35*	36
♠7 6	♠J 10 9	♠9	♠A K 10 6	♠6 3	♠8 6 4
♡Q J 10 7 6	♡K Q 6 3	♡A J 10	♡9 8 3	♡K J 4 2	♡9 5
◇A Q 6 3	◇8 2	◇Q 8 7 2	◇5 2	◇A 8 6 4	◇10 7 6 3
♣A 2	♣6 5 3 2	♣A K 9 8 7	♣A K 7 4	♣7 6 2	♣9 6 4 3

Play Hands for WEST (* = dealer)

1	2	3	4*	5	6
♠10865	♠876	♠QJ	♠A64	♠1043	♠876
♥KQJ10	♥K6	♥632	♥10985	♥A8	♥KQ3
♦K96	♦943	♦J852	♦84	♦KQJ107	♦A43
♣J8	♣AKQJ2	♣AKQJ	♣A1075	♣Q74	♣AKQ2

7	8*	9	10	11	12*
♠1074	♠964	♠102	♠KJ98	♠QJ108	♠A98
♥QJ97	♥QJ102	♥4	♥654	♥QJ5	♥K42
♦K75	♦A2	♦K1076	♦J5	♦542	♦Q86
♣1064	♣7632	♣876542	♣J873	♣K63	♣AKQ3

13	14	15	16*	17	18
♠AK863	♠AKJ5	♠QJ4	♠AJ10743	♠K109	♠AK752
♥J982	♥8732	♥9	♥K84	♥10	♥KQ
♦A9	♦Q94	♦AKQ107	♦A10	♦8653	♦AKJ6
♣Q9	♣J6	♣8642	♣63	♣AK742	♣KQ

19	20*	21	22	23	24*
♠J1053	♠76	♠QJ4	♠J97543	♠108	♠K86542
♥94	♥K852	♥KQ6	♥10	♥6	♥A
♦J108	♦9863	♦K74	♦10953	♦1098754	♦AK54
♣10986	♣Q107	♣K932	♣104	♣Q1087	♣K8

25	26	27	28*	29	30
♠J83	♠A1093	♠K65432	♠7	♠1098	♠KJ1093
♥109654	♥A65	♥986	♥AJ107632	♥43	♥K9
♦KQ10	♦AK10	♦---	♦QJ10	♦87652	♦1052
♣AK	♣954	♣KQJ4	♣43	♣K72	♣AQ8

31	32*	33	34	35	36*
♠Q103	♠875432	♠KQ65	♠Q972	♠85	♠A932
♥854	♥74	♥KQ54	♥7	♥Q9	♥743
♦J1094	♦A75	♦AJ64	♦10973	♦QJ752	♦KJ8
♣KQ7	♣94	♣4	♣10853	♣AK53	♣QJ5